DR. DAMAL R. LOUIS

Strategies of Prayer Vol. 3

Understanding Your Position and Accessing Your Power in Prayer

Copyright © 2020 by Dr. Damal R. Louis

All rights reserved. No part of this publication may be reproduced, stored or transmitted in any form or by any means, electronic, mechanical, photocopying, recording, scanning, or otherwise without written permission from the publisher. It is illegal to copy this book, post it to a website, or distribute it by any other means without permission.

First edition

Contents

Preface   iv

Dedication   vi

Acknowledgements   vii

1   Faith   1

2   Healing   33

3   Vision/Foresight/Insight   62

4   Wisdom/Knowledge/Understanding   86

Preface

There are times in our lives when we may find ourselves overwhelmed by life's circumstances. There may have been a recent diagnosis from the doctor, an unexpected layoff on the job, the repossession of a car, a marriage that has dissolved, the sudden death of a relative, or a financial struggle due to insurmountable debt. But, when life happens, we must turn to the One who can handle what seems to be too much for us to handle! God is our Source and Strength, and prayer is the way we communicate with Him. Through strategic prayer we have the luxury of casting our cares on Him, and in return we receive the peace, guidance and understanding for every situation we may experience. God is not unaware of the difficulties we encounter; He is a Loving Father who wants to be a Present Help in the lives of His children. He has all of the wisdom and knowledge we need to face what lies ahead. He understands our worries, cares, and fears. In fact, what concerns us, concerns Him! There is just one thing He needs from us to move in our situation—that one thing is Faith!

Faith unlocks the door to every promise and provision God has for us. It is the means by which we receive answers to our prayers. It allows us to obtain insight on what God is presently doing in our lives and vision for what He desires to do in the future!

It is our Faith which strengthens us in difficult times and moves God to come to our aid and rescue. As we activate our faith, we must remember that knowing *how* to pray positions us, but knowing *what* to pray makes us powerful and effective!

In this book, you will receive the tools needed to encourage you to walk in the wisdom of God, refocus so God can give you clear vision, and strengthen your Faith to believe God for healing in every area of your life. It is my prayer that this book would be instrumental in you not only developing and growing in your prayer communication with God, but also assist you in maintain the Victory in your life!

Dedication

~In Loving Memory~

To my grandfather…Elder Geroy Carroll, Sr. for instilling Faith and the Word of God in me at a very early age. I thank God for the exposure of a little white church in Waxahachie, TX with hardwood floors, tambourines, devotion, and testimony service…and the tea cakes after church didn't hurt either! Lol I am grateful for our talks about the Lord and your encouragement for me to continue in the things of God. The legacy of preachers continues because of the impression you left on my life. I love and miss you Granddaddy, your granddaughter, Dr. Damal Louis.

Acknowledgements

I would like to give Special Thanks to:

~First Lady Roberta Smith who taught and trained me in the Word of God for over 20 years. I will always appreciate you for pouring into a 16-year-old girl who walked into the doors of a white framed church on Denley Drive in a stonewashed denim wrap skirt. You taught me how to study and rightly divide the Word, helped to cultivate my spiritual gifting, and taught me how to live Holy. I am who I am, in part, because of your love and teaching. I honor and love you.

~My Bishop, Darrell W. Blair, Senior Pastor (New Breed Christian Center) who, for the last 13 years, has covered, encouraged, trained, and pushed me towards the destiny and call of God on my life. I am grateful for the one-on-one time we shared in the Word…even though you are famous now! (inside joke) Lol But seriously, as the watchman of my soul, you have been very intricate in my spiritual growth. I went into full-time ministry and wrote my first book under your leadership, and you have supported me in every transition. God knew just what I needed when I came to New Breed and I am thankful that not only can I call you Pastor, brother, friend, but you all are family. I love you, Pastor LaTonja, the kids and the whole NBCC family.

1

Faith

We all have faith! You may beg to differ, but it is true. Imagine that you are on your way to an important meeting at your place of employment. You enter the room with a report in one hand and your device in the other. You pull the chair out and *sit* down after sitting the report and device on the table. Without any thought, you assume the chair will support you. What you did **not** do is turn the chair over to inspect its craftsmanship! You did not check for loose screws, nor did you call the manufacturer to inquire about the chair's weight restriction. Why? Because you have faith that the chair is going to do what chairs are designed to do, which is to hold you up. Although I used this natural illustration to explain a spiritual phenomenon, the truth remains the same—we all have faith!

What Is Faith?

Faith is defined as a moral conviction of religious truth. It is also total reliance, full assurance, and complete trust. When we have faith in God, it means that we completely depend on Him.

To depend on God means that we have to release control of ourselves and allow Him to be in control of our lives and over whatever we may be experiencing. This requires practice because we, by nature, inherently attempt to control the things that are beyond our control. For example, as much as we love and want the best for our spouses and our children, we cannot control their actions or decisions, no matter how much we try to. We cannot control how others treat us, neither can we control the things that have happened in our past. We can desire different outcomes in these scenarios, but the truth is, we have to be resolved in the fact that we cannot change them. What we should do is welcome the principles of the Serenity Prayer as it states, "God, grant me the serenity to accept the things I cannot change, courage to change the things I can, and wisdom to know the difference." (Reinhold Niebuhr).

In short, we can place our faith in God because He is trustworthy. Right? Many of us will agree with this statement, as long as God responds in the manner we want Him to respond in. But what happens when a bad report is received from the doctor, or your child is behaving rebelliously, or you are let go from your job after being employed over twenty years? Is God still trustworthy? What if the doctor's report never changes, and the child does not obediently submit, and after three years, you still cannot find a job? Is God still trustworthy? God is most definitely trustworthy, the question is, do we really trust God? Proverbs 3:5-6, AMP, encourages to "trust in and rely confidently on the LORD with all your heart. And do not rely on your own insight or understanding.

In all your ways know and acknowledge and recognize Him, And He will make your paths straight and smooth [removing obstacles that block your way]." Since it is impossible for God to lie (Titus 1:2), we can trust that He will fulfill every promise in His Word! Therefore, "when we pray by faith, we are praying that we trust God to do His Will in our lives, based not on our wishes or desires, but on what He has promised to do." (Ron Edmondson) (*Emphasis added*). And we must come to the realization that we cannot dictate to God how or when He should do what His Word says He will do.

Faith is also firm belief. So, the prerequisite for answered prayer is *belief* or *faith*. In Matthew chapter 17:14-21, Jesus and the disciples came back to the crowd, and a man came to Jesus and knelt before him. The man was begging for mercy for his son who was a lunatic. The man had brought his son to the disciples to cure him; but they could not. Jesus rebuked the disciples and requested that the child be brought to Him. Jesus rebuked the devil, and he departed out of him; and the child was cured from that very hour! The disciples asked Jesus why they were not able to cast the demon out of the child, and Jesus replied, it was because of their unbelief. Meaning, their faith was insufficient. In essence, if we do not receive what we are believing Jesus to do in our lives or on our behalf, the issue is never a deficiency of **His** ability, it is, very possibly, an insufficiency of our **faith**! Mark 11:24, NIV, further states, "Therefore I tell you, whatever you ask for in prayer, believe that you have received it, and it will be yours." The word *believe* in this text translates in Greek as *pisteuo* which means to have faith. *(Strong's 4100).*

We can ask God to do something in our lives, but if we do not believe or have the faith that He can and will do what we are petitioning Him for, we will never see it manifest.

In saying that, faith is another one of the greatest assets that a Believer can have, because it always factors in God's ability! The Bible declares in Matthew 7:7, that we are to ask (and keep on asking) and it will be given to us; we are to seek (and keep on seeking) and we will find; we are to knock (and keep on knocking), and the door will be opened to us. Asking, seeking, and knocking emphasizes the persistent and consistent prayer of faith that we must believe God with. This is the confidence which we have before Him, that, if we ask anything according to His will, He hears us. And if we know that He hears us in whatever we ask, we know that we have the requests which we have asked from Him. (1 John 5:14-15). This means we can approach God with confidence, petition Him with boldness and have faith in His ability and willingness to honor His Word on our behalf! "Faith must be definite and specific; an unqualified, unmistakable request for the things asked for. It is not to be a vague, indefinite, shadowy thing; it must be something more than an abstract belief in God's willingness and ability to do for us. It is to be a definite, specific, asking for, and expecting the things for which we ask." (E.M. Bounds) (*Emphasis added*).

Furthermore, faith involves much more than asking God to do something. God has given **us** authority! Luke 10:19, AMP, states, "Listen carefully: I have given you authority [that you now possess] to tread on serpents and scorpions, and [the ability to exercise authority] over all the power of the enemy (Satan); and nothing will [in any way] harm you." Along with authority, we have every spiritual blessing in Christ. (Ephesians 1:3). In understanding our spiritual authority, there are times when we must "decree a thing" for it to be established for us. (Job 22:28). Decreeing is simply operating in our God-given power and authority in the earth! In fact, "decrees are a tool by which we cause the truths of the **heavenly realm** to be manifest into the **natural realm,** so they become our daily reality. For example, we decree healing when we are sick. We decree provision and abundance when we are lacking. We decree peace when there is turmoil. To paraphrase, decrees are a tool used to fulfill Matthew 6:10, 'Thy Kingdom come, Thy Will be done on earth, as it is in heaven.' (KJV). Indeed, decrees help manifest heaven on earth!" (Elizabeth A. Nixon) (*Emphasis added*). In essence, there are times when we must exercise our faith and believe God to move on our behalf, but there are other times when we just need to exercise the authority Christ gave us and speak to the wind and waves *ourselves!*

Biblical Faith

The biblical definition or description of faith is found in Hebrews 11:1. It states, "Now faith is the substance of things hoped for, the evidence of things not seen." Let's look at a couple of other translations of this verse to better understand what the writer is trying to convey.

In the Amplified version of the Bible the same text states, "Now faith is the assurance (title deed, confirmation) of things hoped for (divinely guaranteed), and the evidence of things not seen [the conviction of their reality—faith comprehends as fact what cannot be experienced by the physical senses]." In the Passion Translation, it states, "Now faith brings our hopes into reality and becomes the foundation needed to acquire the things we long for. It is all the evidence required to prove what is still unseen."

In the natural sense, we can "hope" some things will happen, and the truth is, they may or may not occur; but biblical hope has no uncertainty! In saying that, faith is being *sure* of what we hope for and *certain* of what we do not yet see. "Faith is *not* placing hope in the answers to our problems, it is placing hope in God Himself." (Rick Bell) (*Emphasis added*). Faith is the **evidence** of truth! Therefore, faith is a "know-so" and not a "maybe-so." It is the difference in saying, "God can heal me" and "God will heal me!"

To further understand faith, we must continue to look in the scriptures. Verse 3 of Hebrews chapter 11 states, "*Through* faith we understand that the worlds were framed by the Word of God, so that things which are seen were not made of things which do appear." Although, we were not physically present to witness God creating the heavens and the earth, we can attest to the fact that He did, through faith! "Faith empowers us to see that the universe was created and beautifully coordinated by the power of God's Words! He spoke and the invisible realm gave birth to all that is seen!" (Hebrews 11:3 TPT).

Second Corinthians 5:7 states, "For we walk by faith, not by sight." The world declares that **seeing** is believing; but, on the contrary, we as Believers see through the eyes of faith. Therefore, for us, **believing** is seeing! "Faith is not belief without proof, but it is trust without reservation." (D Elton Trueblood) (Emphasis added). So, "faith" and "belief" are harmoniously paralleled, meaning, they go hand in hand. To believe means to mentally accept what is factual, and having faith means to trust what you believe. We can *believe* that a mode of transportation will take us to our destination, but *faith* is purchasing the required ticket and/or fuel to get us there! Plainly stated, if we never act on what we believe, we are not operating in faith.

In John 5:24, Jesus states, "Truly, truly, I say to you, he who hears My word, and believes Him who sent Me, has eternal life, and does not come into judgment, but has passed out of death into life." When we believe the Bible and the God of the Bible, and trust our lives to Jesus Christ, we move from judgment to an eternal destination through salvation—this is all accomplished **through** faith. Ephesians 2:8, AMP, declares, "For it is by grace [God's remarkable compassion and favor drawing you to Christ] that you have been saved [actually delivered from judgment and given eternal life] through faith. And this [salvation] is not of yourselves [not through your own effort], but it is the [undeserved, gracious] gift of God!"

Fully Persuaded In Faith

Restated, faith is choosing to believe. But faith is not just belief; in conjunction with that, it is firm persuasion! To be persuaded means to be convinced and assured of something. It also means to have unshakable confidence. The Apostle Paul states, in Philippians 1:6, NASB, "For I am confident of this very thing, that He who began a good work in you will perfect (complete) it until the day of Christ Jesus." In Romans 8:38-39, Paul further states, "For I am persuaded, that neither death, nor life, nor angels, nor principalities, nor powers, nor things present, nor things to come, nor height, nor depth, nor any other creature, shall be able to separate us from the love of God, which is in Christ Jesus our Lord."

Paul had experienced many adversities throughout his life, as it is accounted in the Book of Romans, which solidified these declarations. The Jews tried to kill him in chapter 9, he was persecuted in chapter 13, they stoned him in chapter 14, they beat him with rods and imprisoned him in chapter 16, and he suffered severe rejection and judgment in chapter 18. Five different times the Jewish leaders whipped Paul thirty-nine lashes with a cat of nine tails! (2 Corinthians 11:24). Moreover, he was shipwrecked three times, often went without food and water, was exposed to extreme cold and excessive heat, and went many days without sleep; not to mention, he carried the burden of caring for the churches he oversaw daily! But even in the midst of all he endured, he remained concretely persuaded in his conviction! His stance was, even if he lost his life, not even *then* would that separate him from God's Love.

We too, must be fully persuaded in our faith! Fully persuaded faith is faith that looks past natural circumstances. When we focus on the symptoms of what we are going through instead of the surety of God's Word, we will waiver in our faith every time. But, when we activate fully persuaded faith, we can experience manifestation and victory in our lives every time!

The Conviction Of Faith

Faith is also firm conviction. In the natural sense, a conviction is a verdict of guilt declared by a judge or jury. It simply means that a person has been found guilty of a crime. Once the evidence against that person is effectively presented in court, and there is no error in the guilty verdict, the sentence is given, and nothing can overturn that conviction. Likewise, we must be found guilty of keeping the convictions of our faith; not allowing **anything or anyone** to overturn them!

When I speak of conviction, I am not referencing the conviction that comes from the Holy Spirit; I am speaking of the conviction of Truth. These types of "convictions are the central beliefs of the Christian faith that are crucial to salvation." (Dr. Alan Scholes). Because these Truths are the very foundation of what we believe, we cannot waver in them; nor should they be watered down. Having conviction simply means we are convinced of what we believe, and therefore, are governed by those beliefs!

In saying that, "biblical conviction is the product of three things that characterize a Believer: (a) a **commitment** to Scripture as one's authority, (b) the **construction** of specific beliefs and convictions based on that authority, and (c) the **courage** to act on those convictions in faith." (J Hampton Keathley, III) *(Emphasis added)*.

What can be assured is that our faith is under attack. Consequently, our faith is often threatened by erroneous teachings, doubt, and unbelief. The good news is, "conviction stands opposed to doubt and skepticism!" (J Hampton Keathley, III). We must do as Paul encouraged Timothy to do in 1 Timothy 6:12. Paul tells Timothy to fight the good fight of faith and to hold tightly to the eternal life which God had called him to! Paul was not asking Timothy to do something that he himself was unwilling to do. On the contrary, in 2 Timothy 4:7, Paul states towards the end of his life, "I have fought a good fight, I have finished *my* course, I have kept the faith." Paul further states, "But I consider my life of no value to myself, if only I may finish my course and complete the ministry I have received from the Lord Jesus—**the ministry of testifying to the good news of God's grace**." (Acts 20:24). "Paul's conviction was that the Good News he presented was true, and that God Himself commissioned him, as an Apostle, to proclaim it." (Fred Sievert) *(Emphasis added)*. We must also maintain our faith and pursue the convictions of Truth, so that we, in turn, will attain a victory beyond *our* faith, which is the eternal life that awaits us.

The Requirements Of Faith

There are several requirements of faith. First of all, our faith has to be pleasing to God. The Bible declares in Hebrews 11:6, NLT, that "it is *impossible* to please God without faith. Anyone who wants to come to Him must believe that God exists and that He rewards those who sincerely seek Him." In Romans chapter 14, Paul addresses some Believers, who in our time, would be considered vegetarians. They had a situation with other Believers who had no constraints on what they ate. The Believers, who were vegetarians, judged the other Believers, saying that what they chose to eat connected them to s in. Paul stated that both types of Believers met the requirements of God; and therefore, were received by God. He challenged those Believers who were vegetarians to reconsider their understanding of sin by defining it by its root; stating, "whatever is not **faith** is sin." (Romans 14:1-23).

Furthermore, Paul shared a similar correspondence with the Galatians. Customarily, the Jews were circumcised as a token of the covenant Abraham made with God. (Genesis 17). But the Jews wanted to require the newly converted Gentiles to follow their customs, as the acknowledgment of their faith. Paul replied, "For in Christ Jesus neither circumcision nor uncircumcision has any value. All that matters is *faith*, expressed through love." (Galatians 5:6).

Our Faith Must Be Genuine

There are significant indicators or signs associated with genuine faith. In essence, our lives should reveal a consistent pattern of godly attributes that represent our faith in Christ. The Apostle Paul encourages the Believers at the church at Corinth, in 2 Corinthians 13:5, NLT, saying, "Examine yourselves to see if your faith is genuine. Test yourselves. Surely you know that Jesus Christ is among you; if not, you have failed the test of genuine faith."

Paul wrote this final letter to the church to warn them that he was coming to bring correction. They had allowed division to enter the church and began to practice the sinful ways of Corinth. Also, the church at Corinth had criticized Paul and rejected his words, suggesting his apostleship was not authentic; added to the fact that they were unwilling to examine *themselves*. Unfortunately, this kind of behavior can still be seen in our churches today. The truth is, we are often more apt to examine others before we take a look at ourselves. But if we take inventory of our lives, and do a thorough self-evaluation of ourselves, we will see that we are either an effective representation of Christ, or an effective *misrepresentation* of Him. Either way, we are effective.

There are a few things genuine faith will **always** produce. First of all, genuine faith will always produce obedience to the Lord. (Romans 1:5 NIV). If fact, it does not just produce obedience, but more specifically, it produces *prompt* obedience! "Obedience is for the present tense; meaning it must be prompt, or it is disobedience.

It respects the *time* of the command as much as any other part of it." (C.H. Spurgeon). (*Emphasis added*). Therefore, we must understand that delayed obedience is *still* disobedience. We must also learn to obey without question or reservation. Because faith is an act of obedience, the more faith we place in God and His Word, the more faith will manifest in our lives, through obedience.

Secondly, genuine faith will always produce the love of God in our hearts. We are encouraged as Believers to be filled with love that comes from a pure heart, a clear conscience, and genuine faith. (1 Timothy 1:5). In John 13:34-35, Jesus charged the disciples to love one another as He has loved them. He stated that this will be the evidence or proof to the world that "you are my disciples." It is the love that we display to one another that becomes the evidence that we have placed our faith in Jesus and represent Him in the earth as His disciples. Subsequently, Jesus' love is the produced effect in our lives, because of the fact that we have patterned our love after His. We are further encouraged to "clothe ourselves with the Lord Jesus Christ." (Romans 13:14 NIV). Meaning, our lives should exhibit the character of Christ, namely the characteristic of love!

Lastly, genuine faith will always produce the fruit of the Spirit in our lives. Galatians 5:22-23, NLT, states, "But the Holy Spirit produces this kind of fruit in our lives: love, joy, peace, patience, kindness, goodness, faithfulness, gentleness, and self-control. There is no law against these things!" In actuality, the evidence that the Holy Spirit is at work in our lives, rests in the fact that we possess His fruit!

We must allow the Holy Spirit to guide our lives so that we do not give way to what our sinful nature desires. (Galatians 5:16). "In view of all this, make every effort to respond to God's promises. Supplement your faith with a generous provision of moral excellence, and moral excellence with knowledge, and knowledge with self-control, and self-control with patient endurance, and patient endurance with godliness, and godliness with brotherly affection, and brotherly affection with love for everyone." (2 Peter 1:5-7 NLT). "For if you possess these qualities in increasing measure, they will keep you from being ineffective and unproductive in your knowledge of our Lord Jesus Christ." (Verse 8 NIV).

Our Faith Must Be Active

Our faith **must** be active and working, meaning, it must be followed with actions that are consistent with what we believe! What it cannot be is inactive and unproductive. Faith left unattended is inactive; and inactive faith is not faith at all. Faith, also, cannot be passive. In other words, we are not just sitting back waiting on God to work. Faith requires *us* to do something! It requires us to *act* on what we have not experienced yet, solely based on what we believe *will* happen.

For instance, I believed that God would give me the ability to birth children even when I was told by doctors that I would not. When my faith began to get very low, I found comfort and strength in James 2:17, NIV, as it states, "in the same way, faith by itself, if it is not accompanied by action, is dead." Or, as The Passion Translation states, "faith that does not involve action is phony." With this understanding, the Holy Spirit instructed me to activate my faith with actions that supported what I believed! I purchased baby clothes, shoes, diapers, pacifiers, blankets, furniture, etc., as preparation for my expectation; and I miraculously birthed four miracle babies! Now, I am not saying that the only way to activate faith for children is to do what I did. Those were my instructions. What I am saying is, our words and actions must correspond with what we are believing God for—they all must line up! In essence, faith is simply trusting that God has every detail of our lives planned out, even when we do not naturally see the way being made.

Since faith is merely trust in action, then faith has to be put to work. The Apostle James posed a question in James 2:14, NLT, stating, "What good is it, dear brothers and sisters, if you say you have faith but do not show it by your actions? Can that kind of faith save anyone?" In other words, he was stating that our communication of faith does not benefit us, or anyone for that matter, if our *activation* of faith does not follow! This means, we must live faith, and not just profess it.

Remember, actions are needed to manifest faith in our lives.

James continued in verse 18 of the same chapter saying, "Now someone may argue, 'Some people have faith; others have works.' But I say, 'How can you show me your faith if you do not have works? I will show you my faith *by* my works.'" In this verse, James challenges anyone who claims to have active faith, without works. On the contrary, our works must be done **in** faith, and not **instead** of faith. There cannot be one without the other!

In verses 20-22, James questioned again, stating, "Do you want evidence that faith without works is useless? Was not our father Abraham justified by what he did when he offered his son Issac on the altar? You see that his faith and his actions were working together, and his faith was made complete by what he did." James concluded his argument in verse 26, by stating, "For just as the body without the spirit is dead, so also faith without *works* is dead." And in the same manner, our works should display the reality of our faith.

To reiterate, our actions unlock the power that resides in our faith. We see that evident in scripture as we look at the ministry of Jesus. He is the author and finisher or perfecter of our faith. (Hebrews 12:2). He is our example! Oftentimes, when Jesus healed or delivered someone, He required *them* to do something. It was the activation of their faith that initiated their healing. For example, in Matthew 12:13, NIV, Jesus instructed the man with the withered hand saying, *"Stretch out your hand."* So, he stretched it out and it was completely restored, just as sound (whole) as the other." Jesus wanted to heal the man with the withered hand, but the man had to activate his faith, by stretching out his hand to receive his healing.

In Luke 5:20-26, NLT, Jesus told the paralyzed man that his sins were forgiven and to *"stand up, pick up your mat, and go home!"* Again, sin was the cause of his paralysis; therefore, Jesus dealt with the cause of his condition before he dealt with the effect of it. And immediately, as everyone watched, the man jumped up, picked up his mat, and went home praising God." The paralyzed man's healing was completely predicated on his willingness to react to Jesus' instructions!

In Luke 8:43-48, the woman who had an issue of blood for twelve years was healed by touching the hem of Jesus' garment. When Jesus asked who touched Him, because virtue had left Him, the woman identified herself. Jesus told her to *"go in peace"* because the activation of her faith had made her whole!

In Luke 17:11-19, Jesus cleansed ten men with leprosy. He instructed the ten lepers to go show themselves to the priest to authenticate their healing. The Bible declares that, *as they went,* they were healed! One of the lepers noticed he was healed, and he came back glorifying God. He fell at the feet of Jesus and thanked Him. The fact remained; he was more focused on Jesus instead of the miracle! Jesus inquired of where the other nine lepers were and said to the returning leper that his faith had made him whole. The word "whole" in this text, in the Greek, translates as sesōken which means to save, deliver, or protect (literally or figuratively): —heal, preserve, or make whole. (Strong's 4982). The lepers were all cleansed and made well, but the difference was the leper who returned to thank Jesus, was made completely whole. Meaning, that he did not just have healing; he also had salvation, deliverance, protection, and preservation because he activated his faith to believe!

In John 4:46-53, the noble man asked Jesus to come heal his son who was at the point of death. Jesus replied, *"go back home,* your son will live." The man took Jesus at His word and started home. His servant met him along the way and gave word that his son was alive. When the man asked what time his son started getting better, the servant told him the time the fever had left. It was the exact time Jesus told him his son would live. The noble man's faith, coupled with his obedience, caused his son to be healed.

In John 9:1-7, Jesus and His disciples passed by a man who was blind from birth. Jesus spat on the ground, made clay of the spittle, and anointed the blind man's eyes with the clay. He instructed the blind man to *go wash in the pool of Siloam.* The blind man went to the pool and washed and came back seeing!

In every instance, these individuals heard the instructions of Jesus; but it was not until they activated their faith in obedience to His instructions, that they received the healing they desired. Again, our faith must be active as well, producing tangible results in our lives. Faith obligates us to produce! Produce what, you may ask? The end result of active faith is the production of *fruit*. God wants us to "bear fruit" (John 15:2), "bear much fruit" (Verse 8), and "bear fruit that will last." (Verse 16). We are to produce fruit "that proves we have turned to God and have changed the way we think and act." (Matthew 3:8 GWT).

Because our faith is conducive to our ongoing fruit production, our fruit must reflect the source of our faith. **Jesus** is the source of our faith! The Bible declares that faith comes from hearing the message, and the message that is heard is what Christ spoke. (Romans 10:17). In John 15:5, teaches the disciples through a parable stating, "I am the vine; you are the branches. If you remain in me and I in you, you will bear much fruit; for apart from me you can do nothing."

To illustrate, think if I had a cell phone that was activated, but it had no battery life. I would be unable or unfruitful in my attempt to make a call. But after connecting the phone's charging cord to a source capable of charging the phone, my ability to make the call would then be possible. *Apart* from the charging source, I would not be able to make the call. Likewise, if we are separated from our source, Jesus, we will not be able to produce fruit in our lives.

Building Faith Muscles

Faith is developed much like the muscles in our bodies. It requires exercise for it to grow and be strengthened. For example, my husband recently strained his back and had to go to the doctor to get some relief. He had already tried several over-the-counter topical medicines, and ultimately, had to resort to taking prescribed medication; but neither of the two worked. He even tried taking hot Epson salt baths to help loosen his tight muscles. He was in excruciating pain to say the least, but again, nothing helped! After his doctor's visit, my husband made me aware of what his doctor had stated.

He told him that unless he began an exercise regimen to help strengthen his back muscles, that it would be only a matter of time before he would be back in his office again, in pain! Likewise, the longer we go without exercising our faith, the weaker our faith becomes, and the more challenging it will be when we try to put it to use.

Romans 12:3 declares that God has distributed to each of us a *measure* of faith; but it is possible that we receive this gift of faith and never use it! In Luke 8:22-25, Jesus got into a boat with his disciples and said to them, "Let us go across to the other side of the lake." So, they set out, and as they sailed, He fell asleep. Now a violent windstorm came down on the lake, and the boat started filling up with water, and they were in danger. They came and woke Him, saying, "Master, Master, we are about to die!" So, He got up and rebuked the wind and the raging waves; they died down, and it was calm. Jesus asked the disciples a simple question, "Where is **your** faith?" In other words, He was asking them why they did not use the faith that He had given them? The disciples had been with Jesus for some time at this point; and they had already experienced the demonstration of His power and His ability through miracles. Being firsthand witnesses, their faith muscles should have been ready to take on *any* storm! But in this instance, the disciples failed to correlate the faith that they had received from Jesus to the situation they faced on the ship. Likewise, what we do with our faith is up to us! Just as with the disciples, every situation we encounter should allow our faith to develop, grow, and increase.

We **must** respond to God's Faithfulness with our faith. It is when we demonstrate faith on one level, and we see God move, that it gives us the momentum to believe for greater. Additionally, we can ask God to increase our faith, just as the apostles did in Luke 17:5! The more He proves Himself to us, the more we should trust Him. Because we live by faith and God's righteousness is revealed in the gospel from faith to faith (Romans 1:17 AMP), we should desire to have a greater level of faith. (Luke 7:9). Greater, not just in the sense of degrees or the amount of faith, but in the ability to believe for the areas that are more difficult in our lives! In other words, the areas that challenge our faith.

Faith As A Seed

We can also look at faith as a seed. In fact, think about the parable of the mustard seed. Although the mustard seed is the smallest of all seeds, when it is full grown, that small seed grows into one of the largest trees! The Bible declares that birds come and make their nests in its branches. (Matthew 13:31- 32). In 2 Thessalonians 1:3, Paul began his letter to the church at Thessalonica by thanking God for them because their faith had grown tremendously. As a result of them consistently receiving the Word of God, they continued to actively grow in their faith. (1 Thessalonians 2:13).

In saying that, the seed of faith may start small, but when it is developed, it grows **considerably! Jesus planted** seeds of faith in His disciples throughout His ministry on the earth.

Then he instructed them to "go into all the world and preach the gospel." (Mark 16:15). He continues by telling them "these signs will accompany those who *believe*: In my name they will drive out demons; they will speak in new tongues they will pick up snakes with their hands; and when they drink deadly poison, it will not hurt them at all; they will place their hands on sick people, and they will get well." (Mark 16:17-18 NIV). The point of these signs were to verify and validate the message that was being preached; and we see these signs evident throughout scripture.

In Acts 16:16-18, a slave girl who had a spirit of divination followed Paul and Silas as they were on their way to prayer. She taunted them for many days. Paul, being grieved by this, commanded the spirit to come out of the girl and the spirit came out the same hour! Furthermore, in Acts 28:3, Paul did not go looking for a snake to bite him to prove his faith; however, when the snake bit him and *he was unharmed,* those who saw undoubtedly knew that his faith was strong.

In Acts chapter 3, Peter and John encountered a lame man who sat daily at the gate of the temple begging for alms. When the lame man saw Peter and John about to enter in, he asked them for alms. The lame man's expectation was such, that he would only receive that which he required to sustain him financially for that day; and the following day he would return to sit at the temple's gate again. But Peter and John saw an opportunity for him to receive much more that day! In verse 6 Peter replied, "Silver and gold have I none; but such as I have give I thee: In the name of Jesus Christ of Nazareth rise up and walk."

Taking him by the right hand, Peter helped him up, and instantly, the man's feet and ankles were strengthened. Peter and John sowed their faith on behalf of the lame man, believing *for* him, so that he would receive the healing he needed. It was quite apparent that these men of faith exhibited signs that their faith was strong; and that the power of agreement was at work in them! With this understanding, we too must allow the seed of faith to grow in our lives, and through the power of agreement, be willing to sow our faith on the behalf of someone else!

The Benefits Of Faith

There are several benefits of faith. First of all, faith gives us access to a victorious life! First John 5:4-5, NIV, states, "for everyone born of God overcomes the world. This is the victory that has overcome the world, even our faith. Who is it that overcomes the world? Only the one who believes that Jesus is the Son of God." For this reason, the amount of victory we will experience in our lives is directly determined as a result of the faith we place in Jesus.

If we are going to live a victorious life, we cannot allow our feelings, emotions, circumstances, problems, our past, nor the cares of this world to dictate or diminish our faith! On the contrary, as Paul declares, "I have been crucified with Christ and I no longer live, but Christ lives in me. The life I now live in the body, I live by faith in the Son of God, who loved me and gave himself for me." (Galatians 2:20 NIV).

Faith Justifies Us

Not only does faith allow us to access victory, but faith also justifies us! The word *justify* means to be pronounced righteous. Justification is the completed work of God through Christ. More specifically, it is God's act of pardoning a sinner, declaring them righteous in His sight. Romans 5:1, NIV, states, "Therefore, since we have been justified through faith, we have peace with God through our Lord Jesus Christ."

Justification is an instantaneous, one-time act, unlike sanctification, which is an ongoing process of purification for our Christian growth. Again, only faith can justify us! "Let me put it another way. The law was our guardian until Christ came; it protected us until we could be made right (justified) with God through faith." (Galatians 3:24 NLT). "So, it is clear that no one can be made right (justified) with God by trying to keep the law. For the Scriptures say, 'It is through faith that a righteous person has life.'" (Galatians 3:11 NLT). Furthermore, it is the justification of Christ which causes us to be saved from the wrath of God. (Romans 5:9).

Faith Protects Us

Faith also protects us! First Peter 5:8-9, NLT, encourages us to "Stay alert! Watch out for your great enemy, the devil. He prowls around like a roaring lion, looking for someone to devour. Stand firm against him and be strong in your faith. Remember that your Christian brothers and sisters all over the world are going through the same kind of suffering you are.

We see faith as a protector when we take a look at the *shield of faith,* the fourth piece of armor Paul mentions in Ephesians 6. Faith shields us from the fiery darts of the evil one. (Ephesians 6:16). In biblical times, the Roman shield was the first line of defense against an enemy's attack. These shields were made of wood and covered with animal skin; and once wet, they would extinguish flaming arrows sent from an enemy. Because these shields were sometimes as large as doors, it covered the solider entirely. When they were attacked from higher grounds, some of the soldiers would band their shields together in a rectangular formation to create a wall; and others would place their shields overhead, forming an enclosure that prevented them from being harmed by any airborne missiles. Even in close combat, the metal knob on the outer side of the shield would be used offensively to knock an opponent backwards.

For this reason, we must remember as we are fighting against the enemy that we are not in this battle alone! We have access to a mighty arsenal, namely, the shield of faith. When we as Believers stand shield to shield, we are earnestly "defending the faith which once and for all God has given to his people." (Jude 3). When we position ourselves in God and encourage one another in our faith (Romans 1:12), it will be **impossible** for the enemy to penetrate our defense!

Examples Of Faith

The Bible declares that Abraham, the father and model of faith, "did not waiver through unbelief regarding the promises of God, but was strengthened in his faith and gave glory to God, being fully persuaded that God had the power to do what he promised." (Romans 4:20-21 NIV). As we take note of the life of Abraham, we can be encouraged to know that God truly wants to bless us! Therefore, we must strengthen our faith through the Word of God if we desire to see results and experience the fullness of the blessings He has for us!

Another example of faith can be seen when we look at the children of Israel. They wandered aimlessly in the wilderness for 40 years, and after Joshua led them out, they found themselves facing the Jordan River. Following the instructions God had given Joshua, the Priest *stepped into the flooded banks* of the Jordan with the Ark of the Covenant ahead of them. They all crossed over the Jordan on dry land. After all, this was not their first opportunity to activate their faith.

In Exodus 14, Moses led the children of Israel out of Egypt, and they found themselves between Pharaoh's army and the Red Sea. Moses lifted his staff, *the waters divided*, then the children of Israel crossed over on dry ground. The difference between the two occurrences is, at the Red Sea they were full of fear, but at the Jordan River they were full of faith! They stepped in the water before it ever parted, and ultimately, walked into their Promised Land!

Do The Work

It is faith that allows us the ability to access our spiritual blessings; as well as being associated with other godly characteristics we should possess. The Bible declares in 1 Corinthians 16:13, NIV, that we are to "be on our guard; stand firm in the faith; be courageous; and be strong." We must remember the importance of continuing in faith, because the reality is, if we do not stand firm in our faith, we will not be able to stand **at all**! (Isaiah 7:9b NIV).

FAITH

Name two or more ways in which you desire to increase your faith.

_____

_____

_____

_____

_____

_____

_____

_____

_____

_____

_____

_____

_____

_____

_____

_____

_____

_____

_____

_____

In what areas of your life do you need to activate your faith?

FAITH

What scriptures will you use to help you activate your faith?

Take the next few minutes to write your prayer of faith. Remember, God has given us all the measure of faith. All we have to do is put our faith to work!

Father, I activate my faith for/concerning…

_____
_____
_____
_____
_____
_____
_____
_____
_____
_____
_____
_____
_____
_____
_____
_____
_____
_____

Father, I thank you in advance and declare it done in Jesus' Name! Amen

Now, it's time for application! Incorporate praying with faith into your prayer regiment this week. Focus on any area where you may be lacking faith and declare the appropriate scriptures in that area. Do not forget to pray the foundational prayers of adoration, exaltation, repentance, confession, and thanksgiving!

2

Healing

When we accept a position of employment, we receive a benefit package that encompasses all of what we are entitled to as an employee of that company. Likewise, because we are Believers, we too have a benefit package! One of the benefits that we have in the package of Salvation is healing! The Hebrew word for healing is *Rapha. (Strong's 7495)*. The first occurrence where God revealed himself as Jehovah Rapha, The Lord who heals, was to the children of Israel in Exodus 15:26. In fact, He promised to heal and restore Israel, His chosen people. To be healed does not just mean to have renewed health, but it also means to be saved, cleansed, made whole, restored, cured, and to be made sound. To say that God desires for us to be healed is an understatement, and to fully understand who God is, we must know Him as our Healer!

God Wants Us Healed

Have you ever heard someone who was sick say they will be healed "if it is the Lord's will?" I cringe every time I hear this because I know that God **wants** to heal us; after all, He made every provision to ensure that we would be healed. So where do we get this idea of adding "if" to the equation, you ask? The majority of people I have encountered who say this, when asked, reply with "the Bible says it." The only scripture reference I have found that could possibly attest to this statement is in James 4:15 NIV. It states, "Instead, you ought to say, ' If it is the Lord's will, we will live and do this or that.'" The problem with using this scripture is that the verse is taken out of context. To understand this single verse, we must look at the full contextual reference of the scripture.

In James chapter four, the Apostle James reprimanded the Jewish Christians who had become prideful, worldly-minded, covetous, and unspiritual. They quarreled and fought, behaving just as those who were in the world. James went so far as to equate them with adulterers, addressing the fact that they were cheating on God! The next section of scripture that includes verse 15 is talking about these same Christians, arrogantly boasting, and making plans without including God in their decisions. James responded by telling them that they should consider what God's will was for them; and allow Him to plan their lives because, ultimately, only He knows what tomorrow holds. The truth is we do not *own* ourselves! We were enslaved to sin, but now we are servants of Christ!

Yes, we have been bought by the precious blood of Jesus Christ. God paid a great price for us; therefore, we should glorify Him in our bodies, and in our spirit, which are God's. (1 Corinthians 6:20). With this understanding, our healing was never, nor will it ever be an "if" with God!

God Promises To Heal

Healing is one of the many promises of God; and again, it is His will that we are healed! God faithfully keeps His promises (1 Corinthians 1:9) and no good thing will He withhold from us if we walk blameless before Him! (Psalms 84:11). We can trust that God will be faithful to us because He has been faithful time and time again. Numbers 23:19, NIV, declares, "God is not human, that he should lie, not a human being, that He should change His mind. Does He speak and then not act? Does He promise and not fulfill?"

To illustrate, this past November our two youngest sons requested walkie talkies for Christmas. They did all the research online themselves to find the best ones. Every department store we visited; they made a beeline to the electronics department to see what walkie talkies they had in their inventory. You see, my husband and I had promised to purchase them a set, and their anticipation increased more and more as we approached Christmas. Because we have made it a habit of keeping our promises, they looked forward to the opportunity of owning their very own pair of walkie talkies. In fact, on the day before Christmas, as they opened their gifts, they both responded, "we knew it!" They knew they would receive the walkie talkies because we promised that we would give them to them.

Likewise, we can intently await every promise God has in store for us! For as many as are the promises of God, in Christ they are [all answered] "Yes." So, through Him we say our "Amen" to the glory of God. (2 Corinthians 1:20).

The clearest demonstration of God's promise can be seen through the redemptive work of Christ. Romans 5:8, NIV, declares, "God demonstrates his own love for us in this: While we were still sinners, Christ died for us." In verse 10 of the same chapter it states, "For if, while we were God's enemies, we were reconciled to him through the death of His Son, how much more, having been reconciled, shall we be *saved* through His life!" One of the meanings of the word "*saved*" in this text is *healed*. Again, God **wants** us healed; but our ability to comprehend the healing power of Christ is imperative, if we are going to *experience* that healing in our lives! God's nature and His attitude towards sin, sickness, and disease is apparent throughout scripture. In fact, healing was **always** apart of God's divine plan for us. Sickness, disease, and death, for that matter, only entered into the world because of sin.

We were created in the image and likeness of God (Genesis 1:27), and God saw all that He had made and said it was very good! (Genesis 1:31). The word *good* in this text means the best, prosperity, wealth, well-favored, bountiful, and well. Therefore, God's original plan was for mankind to abide in that "goodness" in the Garden of Eden; but when sin entered through the disobedience of Adam, bloodshed was required as payment. (Genesis 3:21, Hebrews 13:11-13). "For since death came through a man (Adam), the resurrection of the dead comes also through a man (Jesus)." (1 Corinthians 15:21).

On the cross, Jesus took upon Himself our infirmities and He bore in His body our sicknesses and diseases. (Matthew 8:16-17). The Bible declares in Isaiah 53:5, that Jesus "was wounded for our transgressions, He was bruised for our iniquities: the chastisement of our peace was upon Him; and with His stripes we are healed."

This means our healing is a finished work! When Jesus was wounded for us, He justified us, removing the guilt of our sin. When He was bruised for us, He took on the weight of our sin and the punishment due us. When He accepted the chastisement for us, He secured our peace, reconciling us to God. And with every stripe He received, He guaranteed our healing!

Healing Is Ours

Healing is "the children's bread," which means it is our portion and covenant right as children of God. Because we have been grafted in (Romans 11:17), and have been made partakers and inheritors of the blessings of God, we can experience all that Christ offers, namely healing!

Think back to the story of our sons. Think about what would have happened if they never opened the gift that we gave them? After all, we bought the walkie talkies for them to enjoy, but they would have to accept them, open them, and activate them to do so. In like manner, healing is a gift! We must accept it, open our understanding to receive it, and allow it to be activated in our lives if we are to enjoy it.

What I did not tell you was what we had experienced to ensure that they received the walkie talkies. After arriving at the store, driving around to find a parking space, and pressing through a crowd of people to shop, we **still** had to wait in line to pay for them! While in line, we encountered an employee who, evidently, had a very challenging day. She began being rude to us even before we placed our items on the conveyor belt. It was very tempting to just leave the items we were going to purchase and go home!

What am I saying? I am saying our sons did not know the sacrifice it took for us to make good on our promise. Likewise, God sacrificed His son, and Jesus sacrificed His life for us to receive the promise of our healing. Not to mention, Jesus Himself, was tempted to bypass the suffering of the cross; but thankfully His "nevertheless" disposition gave Him the strength He needed to complete His assignment. (Luke 22:42).

Consequently, healing is just as important to Jesus as it is to us. In Hebrew 10:7, He states that "He only came to the earth to do the will of His father." Jesus healed every kind of disease and every kind of sickness! (Matthew 9:35). In fact, after hearing the news that John the Baptist was beheaded, Jesus went to a secluded place by Himself. The multitude heard where He was, and they followed Him. The Bible declares in Matthew 14:14 that, when Jesus saw the great multitude, He was moved with compassion toward them, and He healed their sick. In another passage of scripture, Jesus was in the land of Gennesaret, and they brought unto Him all who were diseased, and as many as touched the hem of His garment, were made perfectly whole. (Matthew 14:34-36).

So Why Are We Still Sick?

Why are we still sick? I'm glad you asked! In biblical times, it was commonly known that sickness was often connected to sin. In fact, sin is *one* of the reasons why we do not receive healing in our bodies today. There are several accounts in the Bible where Jesus would tell an individual after healing or delivering them that, "your sins have been forgiven" or "go and sin no more."

In John 5, Jesus saw a man lying near the Pool of Bethesda who had been lame for 38 years. During those days, "those who were sick, blind, lame and withered" would lay near the pool, waiting for the water to be troubled by the angel of the Lord. The first person who stepped into the pool after the troubling of the water, was made completely whole. Jesus asked the lame man if he wanted to be healed. Instead of the man answering His question, he replied that he did not have anyone to put him in the pool after the water was troubled. Jesus instructed him to pick up his bed and walk, and immediately, the man was made whole, he took up his bed, and walked! Later on, "Jesus found him in the temple and said to him, 'Behold, you have become well; do not sin anymore, so that nothing worse happens to you.'" (John 5:14 NASB). Meaning, his infirmity, or sickness was caused because of the sin in his life! Likewise, we have to make sure that we are not allowing our excuses or our unwillingness to separate from sin to keep us from the healing Christ died for us to have. The good news is He is still forgiving sins and healing every kind of disease today! (Psalms 103:3).

Another example of sickness due to sin can be found during the days of the church of Corinth. It was during this time Christians became sick and some even died because they partook of communion in an unworthy manner. First Corinthians 11:27-32, NIV, states, "Therefore whoever eats the bread or drinks the cup of the Lord in an unworthy manner, shall be guilty of the body and the blood of the Lord. But a man must examine himself, and in so doing he is to eat of the bread and drink of the cup. For he who eats and drinks, eats and drinks judgment to himself if he does not judge the body rightly. For this reason many among you are weak and sick, and a number sleep (die). But if we judged ourselves rightly, we would not be judged. But when we are judged, we are disciplined by the Lord so that we will not be condemned along with the world."

Because of this, before taking communion we should do a thorough self-examination, looking honestly at ourselves; especially, our attitudes and motives. If we hold on to bitterness, unforgiveness, hatred or have ought against someone, etc., and take communion, then we take it *unworthily*. Contrariwise, when we partake in communion, we must first be sure that we have repented of sin **before** we participate in the sacredness of the occasion.

Even so, some sicknesses are not related to any sins at all. In John 9:1-3, Jesus and His disciples encountered a man who was blind from birth. His disciple asked Him "who sinned, this man or his parents, that he was born blind?" Jesus replied, "Neither this man nor his parents sinned, but this happened so that the work of God might be displayed in his life."

So it is with some of us today, the sicknesses we experience may be as a result of God wanting to show His power at work in our lives!

Furthermore, some of us remain sick because we do not take care of our bodies. Our body is the temple of the Holy Ghost. (1 Corinthians 6:19). But God is not going to make us decrease our salt intake, stop us from overeating, or force us to drink more water. It is *our* responsibility to take care of our bodies. Pastor Rick Warren says it like this, "God created your body, Jesus died for it and the Holy Spirit lives in it!" When we do not feed our body the proper nutrients it needs, when we do not get the appropriate amount of sleep and exercise, or we do not manage our stress levels, we set ourselves up for sickness at some point. It is up to **us** to make the conscious decision to change any habits **we** have that hinders God's healing in our lives. We must be careful not to place the blame on God if our prognosis does not change, instead, we have to do our due diligence, correct wrong behaviors, and be willing participants in our own healing!

Lastly, we must factor in the sovereignty of God. God **can** and **does** heal, but sometimes His perfect plan for our lives may not always end in the type of healing we expect. To better understand, let's look at the Apostle Paul. Although Paul's thorn was not a sickness, we can get a better understanding of how sovereign God is when we view it through the eyes of 2 Corinthians 12:7-10, NASB. He writes, "Because of the surpassing greatness of the revelations, for this reason, to keep me from exalting myself, there was given me a thorn in the flesh, a messenger of Satan to torment me—to keep me from exalting myself! Concerning this I implored the Lord three times that it might leave me.

And He has said to me, 'My grace is sufficient for you, for power is perfected in weakness.' Most gladly, therefore, I will rather boast about my weaknesses, so that the power of Christ may dwell in me. Therefore, I am well content with weaknesses, with insults, with distresses, with persecutions, with difficulties, for Christ's sake; for when I am weak, then I am strong."

The truth is, there are times when God allows a person to be healed on earth, and other times He allows sickness to remain, and they are healed "on the other side." As difficult as it is to accept, God has purpose for everything He does, or does not do, in this case. For those who remain sick, this means it is an opportunity for them to share in Christ's suffering (Romans 8:17; 2 Corinthians 1:5-7; 1 Peter 4:13).

Whether we want to admit or not, suffering teaches us things that we primarily would not have learned otherwise; but it is in these moments that we must draw close to God and do as Paul did and rely on His Amazing Grace. He declared, "For I consider [from the standpoint of faith] that the sufferings of the present life are not worthy to be compared with the glory that is about to be revealed to us **and** in us!" (Romans 8:18 AMP).

Healing Is Not Limited

We can limit God's ability to heal us in many ways, but I am only going to talk about a couple of ways in particular. When we desire to be healed but our faith is not strong, this can limit our healing.

Furthermore, if we are struggling with a lack of faith or unbelief, it hinders the miraculous from occurring in our lives as well. (Matthew 13:58). In a previous chapter, we looked at the Apostle Matthew's account of the demon possessed man. Now, let us look more intently at the Apostle Marks' account. In Mark 9:14-29, a man brought his son who had a mute spirit to Jesus to be healed. The man requested the disciples to cast the spirit out of his son, but they could not. The demonic spirit caused the man's son to have seizures where he would be thrown to the ground, grinding his teeth, and foaming at the mouth. It had even tried to kill him! Jesus asked the father how long his son had been dealing with this spirit, and father said it had been happening since his childhood. The father asked **Jesus** if He could help him, **and Jesus, in** turn, asked him if he **believed?** I can only imagine the father contemplating the severity of his son's condition, not to mention the length of time his son was plagued by this demonic spirit. The father was able to muster up a small amount of faith. And he replied, I do believe; help me overcome my *unbelief.* Jesus commanded the spirit to come out of him and he was healed. We must realize that it does not matter how long we have dealt with a sickness, or how severe that sickness may be; truly, **all** things are possible if we can only believe!

We may also limit God's healing power from operating in our lives because of a lack of expectation. When we think of being healed, immediately our minds tend to veer towards the thought of being physically healed. Why? Because we often equate healing to just the physical. We may expect to be healed in our bodies, but totally disregard the need for healing in our minds.

Since we can only receive what we expect, if our expectation for healing is limited just to physical healing, then we miss the opportunities to experience healing in other areas of our lives. A lack of expectation not only limits God, but it can also make us complacent in our faith walk. So, we must **expect** God to completely, and totally heal us in **every** area, so that our expectation of healing becomes our manifestation of healing!

Although there are countless accounts of healing of the *physically* sick in the Bible, as I stated, that is not the only parameter of healing. We are made up of three parts: spirit, soul, and body. At any time, we may require healing in either one, or all of these areas. First, we will look at our spirit. Our spirit has three basic components; they are *conscience, fellowship,* and *discernment.* "Man's spirit is an inward organ for him to contact God, receive God, contain God, and assimilate God into his entire being as his life and his everything." *(Living Stream Ministry Pub.)*

Healing In Our Conscience

The conscience part of our spirit is the part of us that helps us to decipher between right and wrong. The beginning function of the human conscience can be found after the fall of man, in Genesis chapter 3. When Adam and Eve ate of the fruit from the tree of the knowledge of good and evil, the Bible declares, "the eyes of both of them were opened, and they *knew* or realized they were naked." (Genesis 3:7 NIV). They were able to see that they were naked prior to their disobedience, but now, in their conscience state, they perceived their nakedness as sin, and were ashamed!

We see the *conscience* part of our spirit further depicted as the Apostle Paul declares, in Romans 8:16, NIV, "The Spirit Himself bears witness (testifies) with our spirit that we are God's children." The Holy Spirit does not bear witness **to** our spirit, but He bears witness **with** our spirit, to God, that we are His children. Meaning, it is a joint-witness and a concurrent testimony!

Paul further states in Romans 9:1, NASB, "I am telling the truth in Christ, I am not lying, my conscience testifies (bearing witness) with me in the Holy Spirit." In this portion of his letter, Paul begins his communication with heaviness and sorrow of heart as he deals with the condition of Israel at that time. He states his concern, not out of a personal prejudice against them, but in direct correlation with the Spirit of God. Not only is the Holy Spirit the inspiration of Paul's words, but He also confirms and concurs with the truth of them.

It is our responsibility to maintain a healthy conscience. We can achieve this by confessing our sins and dealing with anything which interrupts our fellowship with God. Remember, sin must be judged; so, when we harbor sin, we open ourselves up to judgment God never intended for us to receive. When we admit that we have sinned, the Bible declares that God is faithful and just; and He will forgive us of our sin and cleanse us of all unrighteousness. (1 John 1:9). But we must also put our trust in God and turn from sin. Proverbs 3:5-8, NASB, declares, "Trust in the Lord with all your heart and do not lean on your own understanding. In all your ways acknowledge Him, and He will make your paths straight. Do not be wise in your own eyes; Fear the Lord and turn away from evil. It will be healing to your body and refreshment to your bones."

Fellowship: Worship Aids In Our Healing

Another function of our spirit is *fellowship*. We first see this function in operation prior to the fall of man (Genesis 3:8), and we continue to see it after the salvation of Christ. (Romans 5:8-11). Fellowship refers to the connection and communion we have with God. In other words, it is the cultivation of our personal relationship with our Heavenly Father. One of the ways in which we fellowship with Him is through our worship. John 4:24, NASB, enables us to understand fellowship as a function of our spirit, as it states, "God **is** Spirit, and those who worship Him must worship in spirit and truth." The requirement is we **must** worship God in *spirit* and in truth! More specifically, **our worship must rest** on the truth of who God is!

Worship is the environment that God lives in; therefore, our worship must meet His specifications. Worship is translated in the Greek as *sebo (Strong's 4576)* and it means to hold in high respect, or to personally esteem and show reverence for someone. **Worship in Hebrew is translated as** *shachah (Strong's 7812)* which means to bow down or to prostrate. When we look at these definitions in scripture, it helps us to understand in great detail, **what it means to worship God.** We cannot worship God with our intellect, we must worship Him with sincerity of heart. Furthermore, we must esteem Him higher and reverence Him greater than anything, and anyone else in our lives. When we bow ourselves before our Mighty God, it validates our adoration for Him, and it signifies that we submit to His Authority.

I came to experience God's healing power in this manner while worshiping in our church service. I had received the news of my infertility several years earlier, but I continued to believe that God would heal me and allow me to naturally birth children. Waiting to become pregnant the first time was the longest, painstaking two years I had ever experienced in my life; and waiting six more years to become pregnant again was even worse! But I maintained my level of faith through worship. I understood that if God lives in worship, I had to get to where He was. Only He could heal my body and change the report of the doctor! I also understood that there was no way I could fellowship with God in worship, and remain in the same condition I was in. Needless to say, my husband and I have four, amazing blessings from God! I prayed and received exactly what I believed for, and entrusted God to do. One of the reasons why I received my healing is because I remained in a place of worship!

Fellowship: Prayer Aids In Our Healing

Prayer is also another way in which we fellowship with God. In essence, it is our lifeline to the Father. The Bible declares that we should **always** pray! (Luke 18:1). But when we pray, we "do not use meaningless repetition as the Gentiles do, for they think they will be heard because of their many words." (Matthew 6:7 AMP). We, instead, are instructed in Ephesians 6:18, NLT to "pray in the Spirit at all times and on every occasion. Stay alert and be persistent in your prayers for all of God's holy people everywhere."

In saying that, God has consistently shown me that prayer works! It is through prayer that I have seen Him heal, not just in my life, but also in the lives of those I have prayed for. In reference to the above-mentioned example, there were individuals who heard my testimony, after I received my healing, who ask me to pray with them concerning their infertility; and I did. In every instance, it was the power of agreement and prayer that yielded the results we were believing God for!

The Bible declares, if there is anyone among you who is sick, they should call the elders of the church to pray over them and anoint them with oil in the name of the Lord. When those prayers are offered in faith, those prayers will make the sick person well; and the Lord will raise them up. (James 5:14- 15). Remember, it is the effectual, fervent prayer of a righteous man that accomplishes powerful results! (James 5:16b).

Furthermore, there are times when we cannot formulate the words we need to communicate in prayer. But, thankfully, in these instances "the Holy Spirit helps us in our weakness." When we do not know what God wants us to pray, "the Holy Spirit prays **for** us with groanings that cannot be expressed in words. And the Father who knows all hearts knows what the Spirit is saying, for the Spirit pleads for us believers in harmony with God's own will." (Romans 8:26-27 NLT). Truly, if the people of God, the ones who belong to Him, will humble ourselves and **pray** and seek His face and turn from our wicked ways; then He will hear from heaven, and He will forgive our sin and will heal our land. (2 Chronicles 7:14).

The Intuition Of Our Spirit

The last function of our spirit is intuition. Although it is often confused with discernment, intuition is slightly different. Webster defines intuition as the ability to understand something immediately or instinctively, *without* the need for conscious reasoning or rational thinking. Discernment (*or the discerning of spirits*) is the ability to test, determine, distinguish, prove and judge between spirits. It involves examining the thoughts and intents of an individual's heart. In saying that, there is a difference between natural intuition and spiritual intuition. Natural intuition is derived primarily through learned responses. For example, when a mother senses that something is wrong with her child, despite the doctor not finding anything wrong. Because the mother, has spent time with her child and knows the normal behavior of her child, she knows when something has changed with her child. As Believers, we cannot rely on a natural intuition. We must exercise our spiritual intuition, meaning we must follow the prompting and leading of the Holy Spirit.

Therefore, spiritual intuition refers to our direct sense of God or knowledge we receive from Him. It is a strong inner inclination that causes us to respond in certain instances, without knowing why. It gives us the signal to move forward with something or someone, or it will signal us to go the opposite direction and steer clear. For example, when we feel the need to travel a different direction to work without the signaling of a GPS or the alerting of a traffic broadcast, and we do not know why. Later, we find out that there was a bad accident or there was traffic backed up for hours.

I have personally experienced this! And oftentimes, in these moments, we are unaware that we have went another way until we have noticed that our surroundings are different than usual. We may even question ourselves saying, "Why did I come this way?" Some people may excuse this occurrence by merely saying "something" told them to go that way, or that they had a "hunch or gut feeling" to, but we have to understand that in those moments, the Holy Spirit is directing our spirit, intuitively, to protect us from harm and danger.

The Holy Spirit guides our spirit, and we must trust Him as our Helper to shed light on what we are unaware of naturally. God's requirement is that His children walk in the Spirit. (Galatians 5:16-18). But how do we do that? We walk in the Spirit by denying our flesh its lustful desires or the things that it wants. Because the Holy Spirit dwells within our spirit, He leads us into all truth. (John 16:13). Meaning where **He** leads, we follow! It is **our** responsibility to stay in tune with the Holy Spirit, yielding to Him as He directs our paths.

To illustrate, in Mark 2, the Apostle Mark accounts Jesus encountering a paralyzed man, who was carried to Him by four men. When the four men could not reach Jesus because of the crowd, they lowered him down through the roof of the house where Jesus was teaching. (Verse 4). When He saw their faith, He told the paralyzed man that his sins were forgiven. (Verse 5). Some of the scribes *thought to themselves*, why does this man say this? Thinking that Jesus was blaspheming. *They questioned* (within themselves) who could forgive sin, except God? (Verses 6-7).

In Verse 8 it states, "Immediately Jesus, *aware* in His *spirit* that they (the scribes) were reasoning that way within themselves, said to them, 'Why are you reasoning about these things in your hearts?' This scripture aids in our understanding that Jesus *knew* what they were thinking in His spirit, not through any outward influence of indication, or by a learned response, but intuitively. Remember, spiritual intuition is what we have knowledge of without *human* comprehension or understanding. Therefore, to fully operate in the intuition of our spirit, we must be in close communication with God, and we must allow the Holy Spirit to lead us.

Another example of spiritual intuition is how we *"know"* that we are saved. Because salvation is not a work of the flesh, k*nowing* that we are saved is the work of the Holy Spirit. 1 John 5:10, EXB, states, "Anyone who believes in the Son of God has the truth that God told us [or has the internal testimony of the Holy Spirit in himself]. Anyone who does not believe makes God a liar, because that person does not believe what God told us [the witness/testimony that God witnessed/testified to us] about his Son." We cannot begin to understand the complete scope of salvation until we, first, **know** that we are saved. Simply stated, we know that we are saved, by or with, the help of the Holy Spirit. "The Holy Spirit enables our spirit to ***know***, our spirit instructs the mind to ***understand***." (Walk in The Spirit Pub.) God sent His son to die in our stead, Christ died on the cross for our sins, and the *Holy Spirit* makes the work of Christ real to us in our hearts!

There Is Healing For Our Spirit

Again, healing is not just limited to the physical realm. In fact, spiritual healing becomes necessary when our spirit becomes ill because of sin in our lives. In Matthew 9:9-13, Jesus encounters Matthew, the tax collector, at the receipt of customs. He instructs him to leave and follow Him as one of His disciples, and he did. In this passage of scripture, Jesus metaphorically compares Himself to a doctor, and Matthew was the patient in need of His healing. Matthew's sickness was sin!

When Jesus was eating at Matthew's house, He was criticized by the Pharisees who questioned why He would, knowingly, eat with sinners. Jesus replied to the Pharisees, "Those who are healthy do not need a physician, but those who are sick do." Anyone who refuses to acknowledge spiritual sickness, denies the Great Physician (Jesus) the opportunity to bring healing to their spirit. Essentially, Jesus did not come for the righteous, He came for those who are sin sick; that they may recognize their need to repent and be reconciled to God!

Another example of spiritual sickness can be found in Psalms 32, where David states how sin had affected his life, insomuch, that it literally felt as if his "bones had wasted away," and he "moaned and groaned" all day long. He further states, "Day and night you (the Lord) punished me. My strength was gone as in the heat of summer." But David refused to remain spiritually sick!

In verse 5, NIV, he states, "Then I acknowledged my sin to you and did not cover up my iniquity. I said, 'I will confess my transgressions to the Lord.' And you forgave the guilt of my sin."

David rejoiced in the freedom that spiritual healing brings! He declared, "Blessed is the one whose transgressions are forgiven, whose sins are covered. Blessed is the one whose sin the Lord does not count against them and in whose *spirit* is no deceit." (Psalms 32:1-2 NIV). Ultimately, God desires for us to be spiritually healthy, and only Jesus can forgive and restore healing to the spiritually sick!

There is Healing For Our Soul

We have dealt with the physical and spiritual aspects of man, now let us deal with the soul of man. The soul can be referred to as the inner man. It is comprised of three parts, the mind (thoughts, intellect, understanding, wisdom, etc.), the will (the ability to choose), and the emotions (our feelings). The first mention of *soul* in the Bible is found in the Old Testament in Genesis 2:7, NASB. It states, "Then the Lord God formed man of the dust from the ground, and breathed into his nostrils the breath of life; and man **became** a living being (soul)." Therefore, the soul is not something that just resides **in** the body of a person, it **is** the person!

In essence, we are living souls which are *housed* in bodies! We further see the soul referenced in Mark 8:35-36 where it states, "For whosoever will save his life (soul) shall lose it; but whosoever shall lose his life (soul) for my sake and the gospel's, the same shall save it. For what shall it profit a man, if he shall gain the whole world, and lose his own soul?" In this passage of scripture, the Apostle Mark emphasizes the value of one's soul; it's worth surpassing the appraisal of the whole world! In plainer terms, to forfeit one's soul in exchange for the world would be an irrevocable loss.

Jesus instructed the disciples, in Matthew 22:37, to "love the Lord your God with all your heart and with all your soul and with all your *mind*." Loving God is considered the greatest and most important commandment that was given. This meant they were to love God with all of their capability and capacity, with all of their faculties, and their entire being. It is the love of God that keeps our soul in good standing. His love preserves us. Therefore, to love God to this degree is our moral duty and our adequate service.

Imagine what would happen if we were cognizant of every word, thought, emotion and feeling we encountered or expressed. What would happen if we were intentional with ensuring that each of them measured up to God's standards? We would experience what the Apostle John described in 3 John 1:2, as he prayed fort his friend Gaius, "that in all respects you may prosper and be in good health, just as your soul prospers."

The reality is, oftentimes our healing is limited because of the condition of our soul! For example, we experience an unhealthy soul when we harbor hatred, maintain a mediocre mindset, or remain unforgiving. This can produce a domino effect in our bodies causing us to become sick. We must allow the Word of God to take root in our souls so that we maintain health in our mind, will, and emotions. For we understand that "the Word of God is living and active and sharper than any two-edged sword and piercing as far as the division of soul and spirit, of both joints and marrow, and able to judge the thoughts and intentions of the heart." (Hebrews 4:12 NASB). It is the Word of God that penetrates to the very core of our being where soul and spirit, bone and marrow meet. It interprets and reveals the true thoughts and secret motives of our hearts! We must pray 1 Thessalonians 5:23, EXB, over our lives, as it states, "Now may God Himself, the God of peace, make you holy in every way [sanctify you completely/through and through]. May your whole self —spirit, soul, and body—be kept faultless [blameless] when our Lord Jesus Christ comes."

Do The Work

Whether it was the woman with the issue of blood (Luke 13:11-13), Lazarus dead four days in the tomb (John 11:38-45), the blind and lame who came to Jesus in the temple (Matthew 21:14), or Peter's Mother-in-Law sick with fever (Matthew 8:14); or whether it was the demon possessed man in the tombs (Mark 5:1-15), ten lepers in a village between Samaria and Galilee (Luke 17:11-19), the Centurion's servant sick at point of death (Luke 7:1-10), or the woman crippled for eighteen years in the synagogue (Luke 13:10-17); Jesus healed **all** those who needed healing. (Luke 9:11). He is still healing the brokenhearted and still binding up their wounds today! (Psalms 147:3). We can rest assure that for every circumstance or situation we face where we require the healing virtue of Jesus, it is ours for the asking. All we have to do is cry out to the Lord and believe He will heal us too. (Psalms 30:2). Even if it is physical sickness, we can be encouraged to know that the Lord will give us strength when we are sick and restore us from our bed of illness! (Psalms 41:3).

What area (s) do you need healing in?

List scriptures you can use to activate your faith for your healing.

List the area (s) where God has already healed you.

HEALING

Take the next few minutes to write your prayer for healing. Remember, God wants to completely heal you of every sickness, disease, condition, mindset, etc. In fact, He desires to make you completely whole. All you have to do is believe by faith and watch Him bring it to pass!

Father, I need Your healing in...

_____

_____

_____

_____

_____

_____

_____

_____

_____

_____

_____

_____

_____

Father, help me to see and receive Your complete healing now. I thank you in advance and declare it done in Jesus' Name! Amen!

Now, it's time for application! Incorporate praying for complete healing into your prayer regiment this week. Declare healing in every area of your body, mind, and soul. Meditate on the healing scriptures in God's Word! Do not forget to pray the foundational prayers of adoration, exaltation, repentance, confession, and thanksgiving!

3

Vision/Foresight/Insight

Every year our family goes to our annual appointment to get our eyes examined. During my oldest son's exam one year, we discovered that his vision acuity was measured at 20/10. Imagine the surprise of being told your son who wore glasses in kindergarten now has sharpshooter vision! The optometrist stated that it was very possible that he had the ability to see 20/5, but he did not have the proper equipment to verify it.

Many of us may have the ability to naturally see, to some degree, even if it is derived through corrective lenses. Granted, we may not have 20/20 vision, we may not see as well as my son, or come close to having perfect vision. But, even at best, our natural vision is still limited, and it does not compare to the Supernatural Vision of God. What we see determines what we perceive; and that perception becomes our reality. Subsequently, being able to see things is a great asset, but being able to see things through God's Perspective is a much more valuable asset!

The Hebrew word for vision is *chazown* (*Strong's 2377*) which means a revelation or an oracle. (An oracle is a message delivered by God to His prophets.) In Greek, the word vision is *optasia* (*Strong's 3701*) which means an appearing. Plainly stated, a vision is an unusual discernment or foresight. It is divine communication from God. Visions can also be a supernatural appearance that conveys a revelation in the natural. In other words, visions are direct awareness of the supernatural, usually in a visible form. In this, there is a manifestation of something spiritual revealed to the senses. In this chapter we will discuss both definitions collectively.

The Components Of Vision

Vision involves sight, foresight, and insight. Having *sight* means to have the ability to see. How we live our lives and the decisions we make are primarily based on how we see things. The Psalmist understood this when he penned Psalms 119:18 "Open my eyes that I may see wonderful things in your law." In essence, his prayer was for the veil of ignorance to be removed from his heart so that he could allow divine understanding to come in. Furthermore, as Believers we are encouraged to see with the "eyes of our heart" or through our spiritual perception and understanding. (Ephesians 1:18). Again, we may see with our eyes, but we have to perceive within our hearts.

What Is Foresight?

Foresight means to have a forward or future view; and the foretelling of future events are called prophesies. Prophetic foresight was used to relay predictions given by God to send warning, give directions, to encourage, and to set order. We see this attribute in operation in scripture through the prophets in biblical times, but we will discuss it later.

Positioning ourselves to receive prophetic foresight is crucial, as it is a method that God uses to release sensitive information to us beforehand. For instance, there was one time, when one of our sons was younger, that he asked me if he could go to the party of one of his classmates. I told him that I would talk it over with his Dad and we would let him know. Not soon after I said that I had a vision of what looked like a party. I was able to see several of his classmates faces who I knew. But then I saw something in the vision that disturbed me. **One of the young men who attended the party was shot.** After discussing the vision with my husband, and we both were in agreement, I had to break the news to our son that he was not going to be able to attend the party. He was quite disappointed, to say the least. He went on to say how unfair it was that he could not go.

The weekend passed and that Monday he went to school. Upon his return home, and quite shaken I might add, he made me aware that a young man **was** shot at the party he wanted to attend! It was in that moment that I understood that God had sent my husband and I a warning by way of prophetic foresight.

God knows everything about every person. In fact, the Bible states that "nothing in all creation is hidden from God. Everything is naked and exposed before His eyes, and He is the one to whom we are accountable!" (Hebrews 4:13). God has perfect insight and foresight which means, He does not just see what we do, He sees the reasons why we do the things we do, He sees the intentions of our heart, and He sees whether or not our motives are pure or deceptive. God is Omniscient which means He has infinite awareness, understanding, and insight. He is Omnipresent which means He is everywhere at the same time. And He is Eternal which means He is without end or beginning. This is how He was able to say to Jeremiah, "For I know the plans I have for you, plans to prosper you and not to harm you, plans to give you hope and a future." (Jeremiah 29:11 NIV). God said this because He knew everything about Jeremiah! He knew Jeremiah's end from the beginning. (Isaiah 46:9-10 NIV).

Hebrews 12:15, AMPC, encourages us to "exercise foresight *and* be on the watch to look [after one another], to see that no one falls back from *and* fails to secure God's grace (His unmerited favor and spiritual blessing), in order that no root of resentment (rancor, bitterness or hatred) shoots forth and causes trouble *and* bitter torment, and the many become contaminated and defiled by it." We **are** our brother's keeper, meaning, we should be so **connected** with one another that we can sense in the spirit when something is wrong. We must also be watchful of any signs that present themselves in the natural, because the "failure and falling back" of just one of our brothers and sisters in Christ affects the body of Christ as a whole!

Therefore, we must use foresight and watch diligently over one another to ensure that no one falls short of the Grace of God.

What Is Insight?

Insight simply means to be able to perceive, understand, and interpret what we see or foresee. More specifically, it means to have keen visual clarity. In 2 Kings 6:15-17, The Prophet Elisha's servant saw that they were surrounded by the Aramean army; but Elisha prayed for his servants eyes so that he would have insight concerning the situation they were in. After he prayed, his servant was able to *see* that "the mountain was full of horses and chariots of fire around Elisha." In other words, he was able to see that there were more **with** them than those who were coming against them.

Having insight also means to have illumination. Imagine dropping a contact lens in a room that is dimly lit. You position yourself on the ground in the area where it landed but you still cannot see it. Every effort made to find it ends unsuccessful. What happens when you shed light in that area? Although it is transparent, the illumination from the light source makes it visible now. In the same manner, godly or spiritual insight illuminates our vision giving us sight **beyond** sight!

Why Do We Need Godly Vision?

There are several reasons why it is important for us to have godly vision. Firstly, godly vision helps us to see the bigger picture as it relates to the things of God. If God is telling us that He wants to do mighty things through us, but we cannot see it happening in us before it actually happens, then we may find it hard to fulfill the purpose and plan God has for our lives. Purpose gives clarity to what God has called us to do, but vision motivates us to get it done! Again, it is vital for Believers to have godly vision. The bottom line is, if we do not see it, we will not do it. We have to "see it" (believe, receive, and accept it) before we can "see it" (manifest and come to pass) in our lives!

Godly vision allows us to have spiritual focus. Our natural focus is what we see day to day, and is it derived from what we often think about from a natural sense; but spiritual focus connects us to the unseen and requires us to operate in faith. What we naturally focus on is what plays in our minds on a regular basis. It is normally what has our attention the most, and again, it is what shapes our perception. But Hebrews 12:2, NIV, encourages us to spiritually focus on Jesus. This is an intentional feat that requires practice, especially in times of trouble. We are to "fix our eyes on Jesus, the author and perfecter of faith, who for the joy set before Him endured the cross, despising the shame, and has sat down at the right hand of the throne of God." Jesus envisioned the joy of pleasing His Father and fulfilling His purpose on the cross, which was to bring reconciliation between God and mankind; and we, in turn, must focus on Jesus in order to please our Heavenly Father and fulfill our purpose in the earth.

Jesus allowed the future joy that awaited Him to outweigh the present pain He had to endure. In saying that, we must also allow godly vision, coupled with the joy of the Lord, to help us understand what God desires for us, so that we are able to endure whatever we have to go through. And if what we are facing appears to be overwhelming in the natural, it is time to change our focus on our Savior so that God can give us clear, godly vision to see things differently!

Godly vision is also what bridges our present to our future. Again, it allows us the ability to see further than where we currently are. We need to be able to look beyond the pain of our past and our present problems of today so that we can lay hold to God's best for us! Godly vision will always cause us to have a forward view instead of looking back. P.K. Bernard says it like this, "A man without a vision is a man without a future. A man without a future will always return to his past."

Basically, godly vision deals with how we see God and how He see us. When we seek to have godly vision, we will always be prompted to ask ourselves these questions. What is God's vision for my life? Who is God shaping me to be? How does God intend to accomplish His work through me? When proper vision is in place, our outlook changes. We see things differently! We begin to realize that where we are right now, is not our final destination. We also begin to understand that God has so much more in store!

Godly Vision Gives Our Pain Purpose

Secondly, godly vision gives purpose to our pain. James 1:2-4 teaches us that should consider it a joy when we experience tests and trials; because when we are tested it produces godly virtues in our lives. God does not allow us to go through without a goal in mind. He strategically allows these tests to mold and shape us; but if we allow the trials, situations, and circumstances to overwhelm us, our spiritual vision can become distorted.

Pain has a purpose. For example, when a woman is about to give birth to a child, normally, there is pain that prompts her to know that she is in labor. When someone has surgery, there is pain that surfaces afterwards, after the anesthesia wears off, that reminds them of their limitations. In essence, pain matures us, if we allow it; and godly vision helps us to see what we go through differently. For instance, someone may view problems and difficulties in a different manner now as a seasoned Believer, than they did when they first came to Christ; and as a new convert, they may view them differently than when they were unsaved. The difference is maturity. As Believers, we should not try to run from pain, adversities, or trials, because the Bible already helps us understand that they will come! But the good news is, Romans 8:28, AMP, assures us of the end result of our suffering as it states, "And we know [with great confidence] that God [who is deeply concerned about us] causes all things to work together [as a plan] for good for those who love God, to those who are called according to His plan and purpose." So, it is not what we go through that matters, it is how we view what we go through that makes the difference!

The Apostle Paul, of all people, understood that we were going to have to suffer at times. The encouragement is that we have the Holy Spirit interceding for us (Romans 8:27) and we are more than conquerors! (Romans 8:37). In fact, Paul further states in Romans 8:18, "For I reckon that the sufferings of this present time are not worthy to be compared with the glory which shall be revealed in us."

"Therefore, we do not become discouraged [spiritless, disappointed, or afraid]. Though our outer self is [progressively] wasting away, yet our inner *self* is being [progressively] renewed day by day. For our momentary, light distress [this passing trouble] is producing for us an eternal weight of glory [a fullness] beyond all measure [surpassing all comparisons, a transcendent splendor and an endless blessedness]!" (2 Corinthians 4:16- 17 AMP). Which means our outward devastation will not supersede our inner transformation, when our focal point is the "glory" that will be revealed unto us. Jesus states that in this world we would experience trouble and have to endure tribulations, but He encourages us by telling us to "be of good cheer" because He has already overcome the world! (John 16:33).

We have talked about having vision, now let's take a look at the importance of seeing visions. Remember, visions are also supernatural appearances that convey revelation to us.

Visions Connect Us to Our Spiritual Assignments

Thirdly, visions come to connect us to our spiritual assignments. When we experience an actual vision from God, it can change the very trajectory of our lives and others! Acts 16:9-10, NIV, declares, "During the night Paul had a vision of a man of Macedonia standing and begging him, 'Come over to Macedonia and help us.' After Paul had seen the vision, we (Paul, Timothy, and Silas) got ready at once to leave for Macedonia, concluding that God had called us to preach the gospel to them."

Prior to this vision, Paul's initial plan was to visit and strengthen the churches he had planted in Asia on his first mission trip. After that he planned to further spread the gospel in other regions; but the Holy Spirit did not allow them to travel back to Asia. In fact, the Spirit prevented them twice; and instead, Paul and his companions assignment was shifted to them preaching the gospel in Macedonia. This became known as the Macedonian call; but it never would have been fulfilled without Paul's obedience to the vision from God. Likewise, God may still choose to use this type of supernatural communication to reveal our spiritual assignments to us today.

Visions Relay Detailed Instructions

As I mentioned before, visions come to relay detailed instructions. In biblical times, prophets would receive the Word of the Lord through visions. Again, specific information, directions, and instruction were given to them in this matter; but this was normally on an individual basis.

Numbers 12:6 states, "And He said, Hear my words; If there is a prophet among you, I the Lord make myself known to him in a vision; I speak with him in a dream." The prophets would relay the words of the Lord they received, in the dream or vision, to the individual or individuals who God wanted them to. For example, the Lord instructed the Prophet Habakkuk in Habakkuk 2:2-3, NLT, to "Write (the vision) plainly on tablets, so that a runner can carry the correct message to others. This vision is for a future time. It describes the end, and it will be fulfilled. If it seems slow in coming, wait patiently, for it will surely take place. It will not be delayed."

Habakkuk's dialogue with God was initiated specifically due to his frustration with the condition of Judah and God's inactivity. Judah was wicked and full of sin, at this time, and it appeared that God was silent. But in chapter 3, Habakkuk asks God for mercy for His people and God promised to deliver them.

Likewise, the Prophet Obadiah declares in Obadiah 1:1, NLT, "This is the vision that the Sovereign LORD revealed to Obadiah concerning the land of Edom. We have heard a message from the LORD that an ambassador was sent to the nations to say, 'Get ready, everyone! Let's assemble our armies and attack Edom!'" Obadiah received the prophetic vision of the destruction of Edom, the descendants of Esau. The message from God instructed Israel to attack Edom, and also insured that they would overthrow them.

Moreover, the Prophet Jeremiah received a vision from God in Jeremiah chapter 1 verses 17-19, NLT, where God instructed him to "Get up and prepare for action. Go out and tell them everything I tell you to say. Do not be afraid of them, or I will make you look foolish in front of them." It was that very day the God strengthened Jeremiah and made him as strong as an unconquerable, fortified city! God told him, "They will fight you, but they will fail. For I am with you, and I will take care of you. I, the Lord, have spoken!" These detailed instructions, along with God's promise that He would sustain him and protect him from his enemies, was all the reassurance Jeremiah needed to fulfill the assignment of God.

God chose to disclose His intentions through visions. Each of these men were given detailed information through a vision or directly following a vision, and they heeded the instructions. Indeed, the Sovereign Lord never does anything until He reveals His plans to His servants the prophets! (Amos 3:7 NLT). In the same respect, it is imperative that we also heed the detailed instructions of God if He speaks to us in a vision.

Visions Gives Us Assurance

Lastly, visions come to give us assurance that God is with us. In Genesis 15:1, NLT, "The Lord spoke to Abram in a vision and said to him, 'Do not be afraid, Abram, for I will protect you, and your reward will be great.'" These words of encouragement came to Abram after the war with Sodom and his allies and following the captivity of his nephew, Lot.

Ultimately, Abram's nephew was rescued, and he experienced the subsequent victory over his enemies! God made a covenant with Abram and gave him a divine promise to shield and secure him from all evil.

In Acts 18:9-11, NIV, it further declares, "One night the Lord spoke to Paul in a vision: 'Do not be afraid; keep on speaking, do not be silent. For I am with you, and no one is going to attack and harm you, because I have many people in this city.' So, Paul stayed in Corinth for a year and a half, teaching them the word of God." Even though Corinth was an immoral city, the vision of the Lord came to Paul to encourage and comfort him while he was there, reassuring him that no harm or injury would befall him.

How Do We Receive Godly Vision?

One way we receive godly vision is through the revelation of the Word of God! Proverbs 29:18 states, "where there is no vision, the people perish: but he that keepeth the law, happy is he." The word "vision" in this text means revelation. A revelation is something revealed by God through the Holy Spirit. With this understanding in mind, Proverbs 29:18 reads, where there is no revelation of God and His Word, the people are unrestrained (lawless); but blessed and happy is the one who keeps the law of God.

This is why the Bible warns against turning away from the revelation of God. In fact, Amos 8:11-13, NASB, states, "'Behold, days are coming,' declares the Lord God, 'When I will send a famine on the land, not a famine for bread or a thirst for water, but rather for hearing the words of the Lord. People will stagger from sea to sea and from the north even to the east; they will go to and fro to seek the word of the Lord, but they will not find *it*. In that day the beautiful virgins and the young men will faint from thirst.'"

Truthfully stated, without a true vision or revelation of God we will not be motivated to conduct ourselves according to His Word. And if we have minimal revelation, we will have minimal manifestation of the Word in our lives. Therefore, we have to be careful not to allow anything to impede our spiritual vision, causing us to miss God's revelation. If we allow our spiritual vision to be limited, it can cause us to change our minds about what God has said all together.

Visions From the Holy Spirit

Another way we receive visions are through the direct revelation of the Holy Spirit! The Bible declares in Joel 2:28-29, "And it shall come to pass afterward that I will pour out My Spirit on all flesh; your sons and your daughters shall prophesy, your old men shall dream dreams, your young men shall see visions; and also My menservants and on My maidservants I will pour out My Spirit in those days."

Remember, *prophesy* is simply a prediction or foretelling of future events, and *visions* allows us to see what God has planned. We must understand and recognize that these are gifts given to us by God through His Holy Spirit, to prepare, inspire, warn, and encourage us.

Jesus states in John 16:13, "But when He, the Spirit of truth, comes, He will guide you into all the truth. He will not speak on his own; He will speak only what He hears, and He will show you things to come." The Holy Spirit is our Guide. He enables us to see in great detail what God has provided for us. He reveals prophetic truths and opens our understanding by making the mysteries of God plain and clear. In fact, there are some revelations that we can only receive from the Holy Spirit. First Corinthians 2:9-10, NLT/NIV, states, "That is what the Scriptures mean when they say, 'No eye has seen, no ear has heard, and no mind has imagined what God has prepared for those who love him.' These are the things God has revealed to us by **His Spirit**. The Spirit searches all things, even the deep things of God."

Do The Work

A godly vision should be biblically based; therefore, a true vision from God will not contradict the Word of God nor His Character! Assuredly, God will never go against His Word. (Mark 13:31 & Luke 21:33). Therefore, we can **trust** the Word of God! Any vision that does not line up with scripture is either from our own imagination or it may possibly be influenced by the enemy. If there is no divine support to authenticate the vision, we can rest assure it did not come from God!

VISION/FORESIGHT/INSIGHT

How do you see/view God?

How does God see/view you?

VISION/FORESIGHT/INSIGHT

How do you see/view yourself?

Does how God see you differ from how you see yourself? If so, why?

VISION/FORESIGHT/INSIGHT

In what areas do you need God's insight or foresight?

List any visions God has given you.

VISION/FORESIGHT/INSIGHT

Take the next few minutes to write your prayer for vision, foresight, and insight. Remember, God sees and knows all things. All you have to do is seek Him and be sensitive to His Holy Spirit!

Father, I need Your insight for/on...

_____

_____

_____

_____

_____

_____

_____

_____

_____

_____

_____

_____

_____

_____

Father, help me to see and receive Your vision and foresight now. I thank you in advance and declare it done in Jesus' Name! Amen

Now, it's time for application! Incorporate praying for godly vision, foresight, and insight into your prayer regiment this week. Write down anything God has specifically shown or told you through a vision or shown you in His Word. Do not forget to pray the foundational prayers of adoration, exaltation, repentance, confession, and thanksgiving!

4

Wisdom/Knowledge/Understanding

Picture it, you walk into your banking facility to deposit some cash. During the transaction, the teller gives you back too much money. You make her aware of the mistake, give her back the money and she recalculates your change. Yet again, she gives you back more money than she should. How would you handle the situation? I can tell you how I would handle the situation because this exact scenario happened to me! After the second time the teller gave me back too much money, I asked her if it was alright if I counted back the change, and she obliged. I kept the portion that was rightfully mine and returned the rest.

While some may have viewed her mistake as a blessing from God, as if God needed to resort to these measures to bless; I saw the scene through the eyes of wisdom. I thought of how her check would be docked the amount of money she was short of, because I knew there would be no way the bank would take the loss.

I thought about how she could be fired if this was not her first occurrence. I thought about her children who might suffer or her bills she might not be able to pay as a result of me keeping the money. I returned the money because I chose to operate in wisdom—it was the right thing to do!

What Is Wisdom?

Wisdom, as defined in the Strong's Exhaustive Concordance, is divine skill and full intelligence. (*Greek 4678*). But let's take a more in depth look at the meaning of the word. Webster defines wisdom as "the ability to discern or judge what is true or right." But it is not just enough to know the right thing to do; wisdom means *doing* the right thing! Wisdom is also knowledge, discernment, and sound judgment which ultimately results in complete fulfillment, lasting joy, and peace.

The truth is, I would not have been able to rest knowing that I caused someone harm or loss by keeping money that was not rightfully mine. The look of shock mixed with appreciation for my honesty manifested in tears in the eyes of the teller that day. She thanked me repeatedly and, honestly, I was proud of the choice I made to walk in wisdom!

Wisdom is also keen perception and divine insight. It is the ability to know what to say, or if anything needs to be said at all. William Scott Downy states, "The difference between a wise and foolish man is this. The former (wise man) sees much, thinks much, and speaks little; but the latter (foolish man) speaks more than he either sees or thinks!" (*Emphasis added*).

In addition, Evan Esar states, "An intelligent man believes only half of what he hears, but a wise man knows which half to believe."

Divine Wisdom Comes From God

Wisdom is a divine attribute of God, therefore divine wisdom does not come from human knowledge, it is revealed only by God. Our human intelligence or education is limited and cannot be compared to godly wisdom. In fact, these can often handicap a Believer if they chose to live solely by these limited resources. One of the main differences between worldly wisdom and godly wisdom is, worldly wisdom tends be more self-centered or self-absorbed, while godly wisdom is rooted in the reverence of God!

God's Wisdom makes the wisdom of this world look foolish! (1 Corinthians 1:19-20). It is by His Power, God made the earth. He founded the world by His wisdom and stretched out the heavens by his understanding. (Jeremiah 10:12). Meaning, God prepared everything *with* purpose and *on* purpose. Every star He flung in the sky, the division of light and darkness, the separation of water and land, and even the creation of man was all done by the Wisdom and Power of God! Therefore, we must not rest on human wisdom, but instead we rest on God's Power. (1 Corinthians 2:5).

Proverbs 8:11 states that "wisdom is far more valuable than rubies, and nothing we can desire can compare with her (*wisdom*)." Proverbs 3:14-16 states, "For she (*wisdom*) is more profitable than silver and yields better returns than gold. She is more precious than rubies; nothing you desire can compare with her. Long life is in her right hand; in her left hand are riches and honor." The writer uses this analogy to help us understand the value and worth of wisdom by relating it to silver, rubies, and gold; these are some of our most precious resources. Although these resources can obtain earthly pleasures, they cannot provide complete fulfillment, lasting joy, and peace. Again, only wisdom can do that. Subsequently, when we rely on God's Divine Wisdom, we cannot go wrong or fail!

Restated, God is the giver of wisdom! In fact, the Bible declares that the Lord gives wisdom; from His mouth come knowledge and understanding. He stores up sound wisdom for the upright; He is a shield to those who walk in integrity, guarding the paths of justice, and He preserves the way of His godly ones. (Proverbs 2:6-8). This means that God is ready to release wisdom to all those who seek Him for it. Remember, the end goal of wisdom is not to acquire academic achievement, but it is to experience spiritual growth through our awareness of who God is. And those who have God's Wisdom will show it in how they conduct their lives! (James 3:13).

God also gives wisdom, knowledge, joy, and wealth to those who please Him. (Ecclesiastes 2:26). Once we receive wisdom, Proverbs 4:6 teaches us to hold on to wisdom, and she (*wisdom*) will take care of us. We are to love her, and she will protect us and keep us safe.

Verses 7-8 declares, "Wisdom is the most important thing; so get wisdom. If it cost everything you have, get understanding. Treasure wisdom, and she will make you great. Embrace her and she will bring you honor." The Bible further declares in Proverbs 17:24 that "a discerning person keeps wisdom in view, but a fool's eyes wander to the ends of the earth." Meaning we must consistently set our aim toward, and continuously walk in the way of wisdom, using it as our compass and guide.

The Components Of Wisdom

Wisdom is comprised of three basic components which are knowledge, understanding, and application. The Bible declares in Proverbs 1:7 that, "The fear (reverence) of the LORD is the beginning of *knowledge*: *but* fools despise wisdom and instruction." The Bible further states that we are destined for destruction because of a lack of knowledge! (Hosea 4:6).

Wisdom Through Knowledge

Having knowledge is important, we all need it for growth and development; but again, human knowledge alone is not enough! Truthfully stated, "those with knowledge are able to collect, remember, and access information. But it is possible to have knowledge and lack understanding. Someone might have the facts, but **not** know what they mean or what to do next." (Hugh Whelchel) (*Emphasis added*).

Again, knowledge, on its own, causes one to be puffed up and arrogant. (1 Corinthians 8:1). We have all met "that person"—the one who knows it ALL. They are the ones who know **everything** about every topic known to man. You may start the conversation, but it is hard to get a word in edgewise once they get started; and they all but suck the life out of you with each word! On the contrary, we should desire to have knowledge, but knowledge itself can become an idol, taking center stage in our lives, if we allow it! Meaning, we can become so focused with attaining knowledge, that we become consumed by it, and miss the wisdom that God desires to give to us.

Therefore, we must rely on the knowledge of God, over and above our human knowledge. Human knowledge is limited, but God's knowledge is infinite! The Word, in fact, teaches us that it is through the Knowledge of God, and because of His Divine Power, that we have everything that we need that pertains to life and godliness. (2 Peter 1:3). Let that sink in for just a moment. We have access to absolutely *everything* necessary for a dynamic spiritual life and godliness, through true *and* personal knowledge of who God is. Because God has all knowledge, He is able to choose wisely every time. We, on the other hand, being even the wisest humans, may have our judgment clouded by personal bias or prejudice. But when the knowledge of God is reflected in our lives, it produces wisdom. That wisdom can then be applied to situations in our lives.

Moreover, we need the knowledge of God to experience His Grace and Peace. (2 Peter 1:2 NIV). At the beginning of his letter, the Apostle Peter communicates his desire for his readers to receive an abundance of grace and peace; but this would only come as a result of them having knowledge of who God is, and of Jesus our Lord. Listen to the requirements. Only those who have **knowledge** of who God is, and **knowledge** of Christ, can experience an abundance of grace and peace!

Wisdom Through Understanding

Having understanding is a necessary aspect of wisdom. "Those with understanding are able to extract the meaning out of information. They 'see through' the facts to the dynamics of what, how, and why. Understanding is a lens which brings the facts into crisp focus and produces principles." (Hugh Whelchel) (*Emphasis added*). Therefore, along with knowledge, we must also have *understanding*.

There are several scriptures that speak on understanding. The Bible declares that he who gets wisdom loves his own soul; he who keeps understanding will find good! (Proverbs 19:8 NASB). The Bible further encourages us to trust in the Lord with all our hearts and lean not on our own understanding; in all our ways we are to submit to Him, and He will make our paths straight. (Proverbs 3:5-6). This "understanding" is not our definition of understanding, but God's!

In Proverbs 17:27, NIV, the Bible declares that "the one who has knowledge uses words with restraint, and whoever has understanding is even-tempered." Have you ever heard someone use profanity every other word they say to get their point across? Or someone who angrily shouts regularly to express how they feel? Or, even still, maybe you are the person who have been in these shoes. This scripture helps us to understand that someone who has knowledge is careful of the words they say and only talks when necessary; and someone who has understanding is calm, gracious, and peaceful. Proverbs 2:2-5, ESV, further states, "Making your ear attentive to wisdom and inclining your heart to understanding; yes, if you call out for insight and raise your voice for understanding, if you seek it like silver and search for it as for hidden treasures, **then** you will understand the fear of the Lord and find the knowledge of God."

One of the best illustrations of understanding is found in Proverbs 24:3-4, AMP, as it relates *wisdom* to a house, *understanding* as the foundation that supports it and *knowledge* as the furniture that fills it. It states, "through [skillful and godly] wisdom a house [a life, a home, a family] is built, and by understanding it is established [on a sound and good foundation], and by knowledge its rooms are filled with all precious and pleasant riches." That word *established,* in this text, comes from the Hebrew word, *kuwn,* which means to be erect, fixed, firm, framed, set up and to be stable. Think about a physical house. The foundation is the most important part of the structure because everything else rests on it. If the foundation of a house is unstable, the house will eventually crumble. And what would a house be without furniture in it?

In essence, godly wisdom builds, understanding establishes stability and knowledge ties everything together. This proverb gives us a rule we can live by and apply to any area of our lives, understanding there are no shortcuts and no other alternatives for godly wisdom!

The Application Of Wisdom

Having knowledge and understanding without the *application* of it, is not true wisdom. After all, knowledge is the accumulation of facts, but wisdom is the appropriate *use* of those facts. Which means, "those with wisdom know which principle to apply in any given context." (Hugh Whelchel) (Emphasis added). Therefore, it is equally as important to apply the knowledge that we have to our everyday lives, as it is to have it! Acquiring information without effective application is merely insight that has no destination.

In the same respect, we cannot unlock the wisdom of God without acknowledging Him as the source; and we cannot operate in that wisdom without acting on what we know and understand. When we consistently revere God, through the knowledge and understanding of who He is, and *apply* the required action in response to what we *know*, we are walking in wisdom!

In the prologue of Solomon's writing in Proverbs 1, he states, "Here are kingdom revelations, words to live by, and words of wisdom given to empower you to reign in life, written as proverbs by Israel's King Solomon, David's son. Within these sayings will be found the revelation of wisdom and the impartation of spiritual understanding. Use them as keys to unlock the treasures of true knowledge. Those who cling to these words will receive discipline to demonstrate wisdom in every relationship and to choose what is right and just and fair. These proverbs will give you great skill to teach the immature and make them wise, to give youth the understanding of their design and destiny. For the wise, these proverbs will make you even wiser, and for those with discernment, you will be able to acquire brilliant strategies for leadership. These kingdom revelations will break open your understanding to unveil the deeper meaning of parables, poetic riddles, and epigrams, and to unravel the words and enigmas (mysteries) of the wise. We cross the threshold of true knowledge when we live in obedient devotion to God. Stubborn know- it-all's will never stop to do this, for they scorn true wisdom and knowledge." (Proverbs 1:1-7 TPT).

Wisdom In Scripture

To understand wisdom better, we can search the scriptures. The Bible is packed with countless examples that we can draw from! For example, it was wisdom that Solomon relied on to decipher which mother was telling the truth in 1 Kings 3:16-28, NET. Let's look at how Solomon responded to these mothers with wisdom:

"**16** Then two prostitutes came to the king (Solomon) and stood before him. **17** One of the women said, 'My master, this woman and I live in the same house. I had a baby while she was with me in the house. **18** Then three days after I had my baby, this woman also had a baby. We were alone; there was no one else in the house except the two of us. **19** This woman's child suffocated during the night when she rolled on top of him. **20** She got up in the middle of the night and took my son from my side, while your servant was sleeping. She put him in her arms, and put her dead son in my arms. **21** I got up in the morning to nurse my son, and there he was, dead! But when I examined him carefully in the morning, I realized it was not my baby.' **22** The other woman said, 'No! My son is alive; your son is dead!' But the first woman replied, 'No, your son is dead; my son is alive.' Each presented her case before the king. **23** The king said, 'One says, 'My son is alive; your son is dead,' while the other says, 'No, your son is dead; my son is alive.' **24** The king ordered, 'Get me a sword!' So they placed a sword before the king. **25** The king then said, 'Cut the living child in two, and give half to one and half to the other!' **26** The real mother spoke up to the king, for her motherly instincts were aroused. She said, 'My master, give her the living child! Whatever you do, don't kill him!' But the other woman said, 'Neither one of us will have him! Let them cut him in two!' **27** The king responded, 'Give the first woman the living child; don't kill him. She is the mother.' **28** When all Israel heard about the judicial decision which the king had rendered, they respected the king, for they realized that he possessed supernatural wisdom to make judicial decisions."

We Should Desire Wisdom

As Believers, one of the greatest qualities we can acquire is wisdom. Divine wisdom has no limitations and no hidden agendas. For this reason, we should desire to be filled with the knowledge of His Will in all wisdom and spiritual understanding. (Colossians 1:9). If we think we are wise by the standards of this world, and that is enough, then we are deceiving ourselves! The Bible declares that we must become a fool, in the sight of the world, in order to become wise in the sight of God! (1 Corinthians 3:18) But what exactly does that mean? The Apostle Paul urges the Church at Corinth in his letter to examine their assumptions about what they perceived as true and what was false. He warns them of the danger of wanting to be wise by the standards of the world. The truth is it is tempting to want to be esteemed as wise and powerful among those in our culture. There is a level of respect and admiration that is associated with that. But Paul's main point was to help them understand that godly wisdom is superior to the wisdom of man, and that becoming a "fool" did not mean actual ignorance; it means having a willingness to follow God's truth even when it is unpopular or misunderstood by the world!

After all, the wisdom of this world is foolishness in God's sight. As it is written: "He catches the wise in their craftiness"; and again, "The Lord knows that the thoughts of the wise are futile (vain)." (1 Corinthians 3:19-20 NIV). The bottom line is the foolishness of God is wiser than human wisdom. (1 Corinthians 1:25). Truly, God has taken the foolish things of this world to put to shame those who think they have attained a level of wisdom that compares to the Wisdom of God. (1 Corinthians 1:27).

WISDOM/KNOWLEDGE/UNDERSTANDING

In James 3:13-17, NLT, the Apostle James makes the distinction between worldly wisdom and godly wisdom. Verses 13-14 reveal the picture of worldly wisdom as it states, "But if you are bitterly jealous and there is selfish ambition in your heart, don't cover up the truth with boasting and lying. For jealousy and selfishness are not God's kind of wisdom. Such things are earthly, unspiritual, and demonic." Verse 17 gives us the guideline of godly wisdom as it states that the wisdom that comes from Heaven is first of all **pure**. This means it is morally and spiritually undefiled, and it is without flaw or contamination. It is **peaceable**, meaning it is courteous, considerate, and charitable. It is **gentle** and patient. It is **easy to be entreated** which means it is reasonable, yielding, and submissive. It is **full of mercy**, compassion, and grace. It is **impartial** which means it is fair and just. And it is **sincere** which means it is genuine.

As Believers, there are attributes and characteristics that we are required to possess if we are to be considered wise. First and foremost, we must maintain a reverence of God. This means that we esteem Him with the utmost respect, and we honor Him with our lives. (Psalms 110:11 CEV). We must remain submitted to God's Will. This means that we obey His Word and line up with His Plan for our lives. (Colossians 1:9-10). We must pay careful attention to our spiritual walk. Meaning, that we take responsibility for our spiritual growth and how we live our lives. (Ephesians 5:15 AMP). We must maintain a level of humility. This means that we are sober in our thinking of ourselves and are not overconfident or arrogant. (Proverbs 11:2 AMP). We must exhibit self-control. This means we have the ability to resist temptation and are able to make godly decisions. (2 Peter 1:5-8).

The truth is we cannot build a godly life marked by success and peace, without having godly wisdom!

We Need Wisdom

We need wisdom, and there are several reasons why. First of all, we need wisdom so that we can experience a long, happy, fulfilling life. The Bible declares in Proverbs 9:11, NIV, "For through wisdom your days will be many, and years will be added to your life." Wisdom makes life pleasant, and it leads us on a peaceful path. Likewise, wisdom is a life-giving tree, and the source of happiness for those who retain her (wisdom). (Proverbs 3:17-18). Proverbs chapter 3 verse 13 begins by saying the man who *"finds"* wisdom will be happy; and it ends in verse 18 by saying those who *"retain"* wisdom will be happy. Therefore, our happiness is not just predicated on the fact that we have found wisdom; but we must *also* continue to maintain and apply wisdom if we are going to remain happy.

Truthfully stated, we need wisdom to effectively navigate through life's journey. It enables us to make sound choices and well-informed decisions. When we are led in the way of wisdom and follow the righteous paths, when we walk our steps will not be hindered, and when we run, we will not stumble. (Proverbs 4:11-12). As we allow wisdom to direct our every move with precision, we can successfully and consistently operate through the course of our lives.

Moreover, in Ephesians 5:15-16, the Apostle Paul warns the church at Ephesus by saying, "be very careful how you live, not as unwise but as wise, making the most of every opportunity, because the days are evil." The closer we are to Christ's return, the more imperative it is for us to rely on His wisdom. So, we continue to preach Christ to each person, using all wisdom to warn and to teach everyone, in order to bring each one into God's presence as a mature person in Christ. (Colossians 1:28). In this way, we are being intentional with fulfilling the Will of God for our lives; most assuredly, we need wisdom to do that.

Lastly, Proverbs 3:7-8 states, "Do not be wise in your own eyes; fear the Lord and shun evil. This will bring health to your body and nourishment to your bones." Therefore, we must fully trust in the wisdom of God, so that we do not have to rely on our own understanding and logic. If we listen for His voice and submit to His wisdom, He will lead us in the direction we should go. (Proverbs 3:5-6).

With Wisdom Comes Favor And Success

Secondly, we need wisdom so that we will experience favor and success. Success is not having the biggest house, the most luxurious car, or thousands of dollars in the bank, it is walking in the wisdom of God! Again, having wisdom involves having knowledge, understanding, and application thereof. When we apply ourselves to learn biblical principles and **do** them, the Bible declares in Proverbs 3:4, that we "will find favor and good success in the sight of God and man."

This means that through wisdom we have the ability to receive *natural* and *spiritual* prosperity! There is a wealth of inherited treasures and significant resources that we have access to when we walk wisely. It is when we operate the principles of God, namely wisdom, that we reap all of its benefits as a result.

With Wisdom Comes Blessings

Thirdly, if we desire to be blessed, we must walk in wisdom. Proverbs 3:13 declares that we are blessed when we find wisdom and acquire understanding. In 2 Chronicles 1:7, NIV, God appeared to Solomon at night and said to him, "Ask for whatever you want me to give you." Solomon replied, "Give me wisdom and knowledge, that I may lead this people, for who is able to govern this great people of yours?" God said to Solomon, "Since this is your heart's desire and you have not asked for wealth, possessions or honor, nor for the death of your enemies, and since you have not asked for a long life but for wisdom and knowledge to govern my people over whom I have made you king, therefore wisdom and knowledge will be given you. **And** I will also give you wealth, possessions, and honor, such as no king who was before you ever had and none after you will have." (Verses 10-12). Solomon was blessed with more than his heart desired simply because he asked God for wisdom!

Walking in wisdom also means that we have privileged information. We are made aware of the dangers and pitfalls that are ahead of us, as well as the opportunities and blessings that God has in store for us.

Those who trust in their own insight are foolish, but those who walk in wisdom are kept safe. (Proverbs 28:26).

In addition, the Bible declares that "wisdom will save you from the ways of wicked men, from men whose words are perverse, who have left the straight paths to walk in dark ways." (Proverbs 2:12-13 NIV). On the contrary, walking in wisdom is not about how much we can add to our knowledge; but it is about allowing God's truth to change how we think, how we act, and how we live.

Wisdom Gives Us Strength And Power

Fourthly, wisdom gives us strength and power. Job 12:13 states, "True wisdom and power are found in God; counsel and understanding are His." We are therefore empowered when we rely on the wisdom of God. The Bible declares, it is wisdom which makes one wise person more powerful than ten rulers in a city. (Ecclesiastes 7:19 NIV).

God is all-wise, all-seeing, and all-knowing. He knows everything about everything, including the very details of our lives! He knows every circumstance we will face and how we should handle them. Even when we feel we are deficient in power and devoid of strength, He gives us the wisdom we need to make it through. Proverbs 24:5 declares, "A wise man is strong; yes, a man of knowledge increases in strength."

Wisdom Paves The Way For Honor And Glory

Lastly, wisdom allows us to remain in a place of honor and glory. Proverbs 3:35 declares, "The wise shall inherit glory (honor): but shame shall be the promotion of fools." Furthermore, when we pursue wisdom, we are rewarded with "a garland of grace and a crown of glory upon our heads." (Proverbs 4:9). Meaning, we are adorned with justifying grace and glory as a sign of dignity and honor. Indeed, there are blessings that await us when we choose to walk in the wisdom of God.

How Do We Obtain Wisdom?

Wisdom can be obtained in several different ways. First of all, we can receive wisdom if we ask for it. It is given to us as a gift from God! James 1:5, NET, states, "But if anyone is deficient in wisdom, he should ask God, who gives to all generously and without reprimand, and it will be given to him." Remember, Solomon, the wisest man who ever lived, prayed, and asked God for wisdom after being appointed as king. He understood that the responsibility of leading God's people would require more than his ability; especially if he was going to lead them well. We too must understand that if we are going to do anything well for God, we **must** have and use wisdom.

Wisdom From Studying God's Word

Secondly, wisdom can be gained through studying and activating the Word of God. Notice I said *studying* and *activating* the Word. Remember, we have to know the Word and do what it requires, for wisdom to be in effect. Psalms 19:7 states, "The law of the Lord is perfect, refreshing the soul. The statutes of the Lord are trustworthy, making wise the simple." Moreover, 2 Timothy 3:15, AMP, states, "you have known the sacred writings (Hebrew Scriptures) which are able to give you the wisdom that leads to salvation through faith which is in Christ Jesus [surrendering your entire self to Him and having absolute confidence in His wisdom, power and goodness]."

When we feed our souls through the word of God, we can be assured that the wisdom that we receive will come forth in the words in which we speak. We must study to show ourselves approved unto God, as a worker who does not need to be ashamed, teaching the message of truth accurately! (2 Timothy 2:15). We must also remember that "the lips of the righteous feed *and* guide many, but fools [who reject God and His wisdom] die for lack of understanding." (Proverbs 10:21 AMP)

Furthermore, Solomon states, "My son, let not them (my teachings) depart from thine eyes: keep sound wisdom and discretion: So shall they be life unto thy soul, and grace to thy neck." (Proverbs 3:21-22). If we guard all that we learn from scripture, keeping the Word before our eyes and meditating on it in our hearts and minds, we too will experience the benefits of a life influenced and empowered by God's Wisdom!

Wisdom Through A Relationship With Jesus Christ

Thirdly, we receive wisdom as we entrust our lives to Christ. The Bible declares in 1 Corinthians 1:24 that Christ, in fact, is the Wisdom of God! Therefore, we come to know the Wisdom of Christ because we have a relationship with Him, and we continue to have His mindset. (1 Corinthians 2:16). Luke 2:52 states that Jesus matured and increased in wisdom and knowledge, so much so, that He amazed and astounded the doctors and instructors who heard Him teach in the temple. We must also continue to grow in the Grace and Knowledge of our Lord and Savior Jesus Christ (2 Peter 3:18); as we remember that all of the treasures of wisdom and knowledge are hidden in Him! (Colossians 2:3). Matthew Henry comments, "The treasures of wisdom are not hidden from us, but **for** us, in Christ." Subsequently, the truth remains, we cannot live wisely without Him.

Wisdom From Following The Holy Spirit's Leading

Fourthly, we receive wisdom as we follow the leading and instruction of the Holy Spirit. Job 32:8, NIV, states, "But it is the spirit in a person, the breath of the Almighty, that gives them understanding (wisdom). In 1 Corinthians 12:7-8, the Apostle Paul states that we all have been given spiritual gifts, "but the manifestation of the (Holy) Spirit is given to every man to profit withal. For to one is given by the Spirit the word of wisdom; to another the word of knowledge by the same Spirit." This simply means that the Holy Spirit manifests Himself in us, enabling and activating us with the ability to speak words of wisdom as He prompts us.

In 1 Corinthians 2:13-16, NLT, Paul further states, "When we tell you these things, we do not use words that come from human wisdom. Instead, we speak words given to us by the (Holy) Spirit, using the Spirit's words to explain spiritual truths. But people who aren't spiritual can't receive these truths from God's Spirit. It all sounds foolish to them and they can't understand it, for only those who are spiritual can understand what the Spirit means. Those who are spiritual can evaluate all things, but they themselves cannot be evaluated by others. For, 'Who can know the Lord's thoughts? Who knows enough to teach him?' But we understand these things, for we have the mind of Christ."

Isaiah 11:2, NASB, states, *"The Spirit of the LORD* will rest on Him (Jesus), The spirit of wisdom and understanding, The spirit of counsel and strength, The spirit of knowledge and the fear of the LORD." In this passage of scripture, the Prophet Isaiah prophesy, "There shall come forth a Rod from the stem of Jesse, and a Branch shall grow out of his roots." (Verse 1). We understand by this verse and the verses that follow, that he is speaking of the life, character, and ministry of Jesus Christ. Again, the Holy Spirit empowers with wisdom, knowledge and understanding; and if Jesus was dependent on the Holy Spirit to complete His assignment in the earth, we must be spirit-dependent too. Indeed, we need the Holy Spirit's Wisdom!

Wisdom Through Godly Counsel

Lastly, we receive wisdom through godly counsel. Proverbs 13:10, NIV, declares, "Where there is strife, there is pride, but wisdom is found in those who take advice."

Listening to the advice of someone who has the godly wisdom we need is imperative! Our parents, grandparents, pastor, mentor, etc. can shed light and insight on life's journey. They have life experience and have already been where we are trying to go. Furthermore, Proverbs 1:5, AMP, states, "The wise will hear and increase their learning, and the person of understanding will acquire wise counsel *and* the skill [to steer his course wisely and lead others to the truth]." The Bible declares, the lips of a priest should teach knowledge, and people should seek instruction from his mouth, for he is the messenger of the Lord of hosts. (Malachi 2:7).

Moreover, Proverbs 19:20, AMP, states, "Listen to counsel, receive instruction, *and* accept correction; that you may be wise in the time to come." Instruction is the communication of right principles, counsel is the advice by which we practically apply these principles, and correction is the discipline given to ensure these principles are carried out. The bottom line is we have to be willing to be taught, advised, and even reproved, if necessary, so that we can become wiser in the end!

It is a true statement that close association brings about assimilation. In other words, we become what we surround ourselves with. If we keep company with the wise, we will become wise, but if we associate with fools, we will suffer harm. (Proverbs 13:20). Plainly stated, if we spend time with those who are wise, we stand a better chance of making wise decisions; but, if we fraternize with those who are foolish, it is inevitable that we will make poor choices.

Do The Work

Ultimately, we should grow in the wisdom, knowledge, and understanding of who God is. The Apostle Paul writes to the church at Ephesus telling them that he was praying that God would give them spiritual wisdom, insight, and revelation so that they would grow in the knowledge of God. (Ephesians 1:16-17). Although wisdom is readily available and accessible, it requires our initiation; meaning, we must actively pursue it and maintain it to benefit from its reward. Yes, we are traveling on this road called life, but if we have God's wisdom, the way is already paved!

What areas in your life do you need to rely more on God's wisdom?

How do you plan on activating the wisdom of God in your life?

In what ways have you seen wisdom exemplified in the people you are connected to?

WISDOM/KNOWLEDGE/UNDERSTANDING

Take the next few minutes to write your prayer for wisdom, knowledge, and understanding. Remember, God has all knowledge and wisdom. All you have to do is ask Him for it!

Father, I need Your wisdom...

_____

_____

_____

_____

_____

_____

_____

_____

_____

_____

_____

_____

_____

_____

_____

Father, I thank you in advance and declare it done in Jesus' Name! Amen

Now, it's time for application! Incorporate praying for God's Wisdom, Knowledge, and Understanding into your prayer regiment this week. Take note of how your actions and responses differ after seeking the Wisdom of God. Do not forget to pray the foundational prayers of adoration, exaltation, repentance, confession, and thanksgiving!

Made in the USA
Middletown, DE
04 October 2023